IN PRAISE OF
PROGRESS, NOT PERFECTION

This delightful book provides EVERY parent the opportunity to see their triumphs and struggles in the pages of this readable text. To take on the dance of parenting with a child who has differences outside the norm can at times make one wish they had an encyclopedia of wisdom for guidance. The Thompson's have provided just that in their presentation of an open and honest representation of the challenges they have faced. I've seen them just as the book outlines: trusting each other, committed to each other and their children, resilient, focused on all aspects of health, especially their emotional health, and at all times staying upbeat and optimistic. Give yourself a gift and a place to take a deep breath and a chuckle while learning invaluable marital and parenting tips from the pages of Progress, Not Perfection.

Jeri Fitzpatrick, M.D.
Board Certified in Psychiatry and Child and
Adolescent Psychiatry, Private Practice

"This book walks a parent through the joys and struggles of navigating life with three challenging children, while maintaining a healthy and loving marriage. Roy and Margrey share how they dealt with the many challenges of parenting, using realistic and practical strategies while fostering a love for each other and building positive character traits in their children. Through their story, you will gain an understanding of how

Margrey and Roy's wise choices over the past 30 years have helped them to raise their children to be kind and lovable adults. This book will give hope to any parent desiring to raise healthy adults while maintaining a healthy relationship."

Dr. Jane N. Hannah
Head of the Upper School at
Currey Ingram Academy,
Brentwood, Tennessee

"What a refreshing, honest, and practical resource for families who face challenges—namely, all of us! Margrey and Roy have not only written a great book about strong families. They themselves have actually built a strong family. Rarely does one get such an insightful book from a couple who, after more than forty years of marriage, love each other more today than ever. This book is for every family. Get it. Read it."

Dr. David Young
Minister, Author,
Host of the New Day Television Program

PROGRESS
not perfection

PROGRESS
not perfection

Building a Powerful Marriage While

Raising Challenging Children

MARGREY THOMPSON, P.T.

ROY THOMPSON, D.D.S.

HybridGlobal
PUBLISHING

Published by
Hybrid Global Publishing
301 E. 57th Street, 4th floor
New York, NY 10022

Manufactured in the United States of America,
or in the United Kingdom when distributed elsewhere.

Roy and Margrey Thompson
Progress, Not Perfection:
Building a Powerful Marriage while Raising Challenging Children
ISBN: 978-1-948181-99-0
ebook ISBN: 978-1-948181-98-3
LCCN: 2019919839

Cover design by: Natasha Clawson
Copyediting by: Lara Kennedy
Author photograph by: Alan Loveless
Interior design: Medlar Publishing Solutions Pvt Ltd., India

www.margreyroybooks.com/

DEDICATION

Through the years, Margrey has talked to dozens of parents struggling to find their way in the challenging world of raising a special needs child and ultimately find successful paths for their special needs children. In every instance, she has encountered a parent or parents needing to hear that they are not alone and that the craziness of their life is similar to others—and that, in some way, they will succeed over time.

We have not made our journey alone. Through the years, multiple nannies have been a part of our family and of our success. We've had teachers that have been understanding and helpful. We've had the support of principals throughout our children's years in school. Our friends, families, and parents have understood and assisted. We've had several psychologists and psychiatrists, as well as pediatricians, assist in our parental journey. We've even had law enforcement officers who helped us brave the storms. On several occasions, our employees have come to our rescue. This is a testament to the fact that it does take a community to raise a child, and it is healthy to ask for help. We thank everyone, including all those that may have been left out of this list, for keeping us sane and keeping our children safe. Each of you has contributed to our successful and fulfilling marriage by helping with our children.

This book is dedicated to parents everywhere who are rearing children and staying committed to each other. This dedication goes out to single parents, grandparents, and family members who have succeeded in staying mentally and physically healthy and positive as they parent difficult children. Parenting is the hardest job in the world. There are no guarantees on your parenting trail. Some parenting ideas are hit and miss and only stick with just the right child. Some ideas are just plain pitiful—and we've tried many of them. Regardless, this book is a testament and a salute to those parents that endure, tough it out, stick together, and develop an attitude of perseverance.

For years, friends have said, "You two should write a book about parenting and marriage." Words like that are meant as a compliment, but they just got brushed aside in our busy lives. Then one day my colleague, Clifton Simmons, pulled me aside and flat-out said, "Roy, you *must* write this book. Start today!" Thank you, Clifton.

And lest you think that I did this alone, Margrey has had 80 percent of the responsibility of rearing our children. I delegated parenting most days and went to the office to practice dentistry. Most of the stories and all of the best lessons on parenting come from Margrey. Many days I just watched her in amazement. We can't imagine life without each other. We pray daily for each other's health so that God doesn't leave only one of us to complete this task alone.

We have many to thank for our success thus far. First, we are grateful that our parents raised us both with similar value systems. Similar beliefs have helped sustain our marriage. We thank God often that He brought us together for the purpose of rearing our three children. Lastly, we have to thank our children—Heather, Dylan, and Molly—each of whom has enriched our lives in so many ways and given us room to grow and without whom this book would not exist.

Enjoy our stories, our children, and our family lunacy; see what has and hasn't worked; and know there is hope ahead of you. Thank you for joining us on this wonderful journey called life.

TABLE OF CONTENTS

INTRODUCTION

ROY

Trust yourself. You know more than you think you do.
—Benjamin Spock, MD, famed pediatrician
and author of Baby and Child Care

Ah, time to relax. So nice to have a few minutes to sip on a cup of coffee in a quiet room, in your favorite chair, maybe read for a few minutes—or better yet, catch a short power nap.

Yeah, *right.*

"Relaxed" is a word rarely used by the parent of a special needs child. "Relaxed" does not describe the *life* of a parent with a special needs child. "Relaxed" is when you lie down at night and finally get to shut your eyes and sleep—and that's *if* your child chooses to lie down and rest themselves. But before you think family life with a special needs child is bleak, let us reassure you that rearing a more difficult child is rewarding as well as challenging.

Over the last twenty-five years, my wife and I have met hundreds of parents of special needs children. They come to us with weary eyes and notebooks full of questions. Our hearts break each time we meet with a new friend and fellow struggler. Sometimes, the mom or dad appears lost.

Bottom line: At some point on the special needs journey, each of us gets lost. We wrote this book to help parents like you find a path you can walk. We can't prevent problems from occurring, but we believe we can help you endure them and even avoid them. Above all, we offer this book to give you hope and to encourage you as you head into the future.

You will grow and stretch. Your hearts will sing—and break—time and time again. One day you will come to measure your child's success and progress with a different ruler. You will learn to develop your own ruler, not the one other parents and experts use.

We are not suggesting you lower the goals and aspirations you have for your child or accept mediocrity. Your special needs child can astound you! But to keep your sanity, you must build a toolbox. Reality will be one of your most often-used tools. The emotions you feel—and how you handle them—are other tools. Another of your most valuable tools will be your gut instinct.

No one knows your child better than you. Have you heard grandparents on both sides say, "That child needs more discipline"? Even though you love your parents and in-laws, and they truly mean well, they are clueless about what you are dealing with twenty-four hours a day, seven days a week. Pediatricians also sometimes offer only minimal help; they only spend a few minutes with your child a few times a year. The teacher looks at you like you are speaking a foreign language when you discuss how to motivate and lead your child. You will learn to become the educator, while the teachers, administrators, and sometimes even your physicians will become your students. You will also come to depend on the right psychologist or psychiatrist. Invest the time to find them, hold them tight with the tenacity of a bulldog, and ask thousands of questions, like a seasoned detective, to make your decisions. Realize this: Others have walked in your shoes. No, you are not alone in this process. We promise there are other parents in similar—and worse—situations than the ones you have with your child. No matter what tools you use, no matter who is helping you, never forget that your greatest asset is your spouse.

Throughout this book, we will share some habits, beliefs, and disciplines that have helped us to stay positive and raise our three special needs children without tearing each other down. We pray that you and your spouse come to serve as each other's greatest allies in your parenting journey. Our children's physicians have told us on more than one occasion that their job is to support us and cheer us on so we can in turn stay healthy enough to guide our children and give them hope and encouragement. We also hope to bring some humor to the dilemmas of parenting any child, but especially a special needs child. Without humor, your marriage cannot survive the challenges of parenting.

During the process of writing this book, we have struggled with the perfect title to show that this is a book about marriage and about parenting special needs children. We hope the title we chose catches the essence of the topics we'll discuss. We want anyone raising a child—parent, single parent, noncustodial parent, aunt or uncle, or grandparent— to find hope within these pages. Parenting a special needs child is utterly exhausting yet overwhelm-

Your success as a team will take a foundation built on trust, commitment, health, resilience, and optimism.

ingly rewarding. Regarding our parenting philosophies, over time we have come to think similarly. To do so otherwise would bring disappointment and desperation—not only in parenting but in our marriage. This is our reality. Welcome to it.

There are so many books you can read about marriage and parenting. You can find a book that will reinforce what you are doing as correct and, just as likely, another that will make you feel like a "bad, bad parent" or an "inadequate and uncaring spouse." We've attempted to focus this book on the need to be a team that cannot be divided. Your success as a team will take a foundation built on trust, commitment, health, resilience, and optimism.

We have no illusions that either one of us is even near perfect, either as a parent or as a spouse. What we discuss in these pages has worked for us and kept us sane. We pray some words within the covers of this book will add inventory to your chest of parenting tools while keeping the two of you focused on each other as well. As you read through this book, we will drift from marriage to parenting and back. For us, the two are inseparable. Strength in marriage will translate into strength in parenting. You can stand tall, be tightly bound to your spouse, smile, and laugh; enjoy terabytes of wonderful memories; and remain dedicated to and proud of your special child and your marriage.

It is possible. There is hope.

Regarding that nap, coffee break, or book, though, we suggest you buy a really good bed with excellent pillows and sheets—because when you do get the opportunity to sleep, you want and need regenerative sleep. Tomorrow comes quickly.

CHAPTER 1

OUR STORY

Once you start recognizing the truth of your story, finish the story.
It happened but you're still here, you're still capable, powerful, you're
not your circumstance. It happened and you made it through. You're
still fully equipped with every single tool you need to fulfill your purpose.
—Steve Maraboli

MARGREY

Our credentials and educational accomplishments are areas that gave Roy and me the confidence to accept the challenge of raising our three special needs children. In medicine, you are first taught "normal" anatomy and body or behavioral development for this reason. As a clinician, you have to recognize or identify "normal" anatomy before you can identify "abnormal" anatomy. You need to recognize the standard physical development of a child as it reaches certain ages. You need to recognize certain behavioral habits that all children have if they are developing as expected.

If I look at a hundred x-rays of thigh bones, I learn that they look very similar. When I then look at an x-ray where a thigh bone is broken into pieces or displaced or even features an abnormal growth pattern, I realize there is a problem; a diagnosis needs to be made and treatment potentially recommended. Being able to negotiate physical and mental health development in children using medical terms, as well as recognizing abnormal behavior, gave us more knowledge than most parents start out with. Our patience tended to increase when we realized what level the children were functioning at on an emotional, social, and behavioral level and what activities we should encourage to boost them to the next level in these areas of growth.

Roy graduated from Austin Peay State University in Clarksville, Tennessee, in 1975, having majored in predental studies and chemistry. He graduated from the University of Tennessee's Health Science Center College of Dentistry in 1978. I graduated from the University of Tennessee's Health Science Center Department of Physical Therapy in 1976. While working my first professional job at Arlington State Developmental Center, I started my Master of Education degree at the University of Memphis, attending classes at night. A month before our wedding in 1978, I completed my degree in special education and vocational rehabilitation.

Our wedding story begins like everyone else's. It is likely similar to your own story. Roy was in dental school, and I was in physical therapy school in Memphis, Tennessee. One year into physical therapy school, the physical therapy students took a physiology class along with the dental students. Roy was always making class announcements, so I knew who he was when one of my classmates told me that "this guy" was asking questions about me. We dated, and soon I went away for internships, but we kept in contact. After my graduation, I returned to Memphis and started my first job as a physical therapist. Life was busy and fun. I had also started my master's program, attending classes at night, so Roy and I only had time for long evening phone conversations and an occasional Saturday night date or short visit on Sunday. Roy graduated from dental school in June, and I finished my master's degree in July. We were engaged and got married that August, in 1978. Roy decided to join a dental practice with an older dentist who was losing his eyesight, and we moved to Murfreesboro, Tennessee.

We'd married and moved to a strange new town, and after the honeymoon, Roy began practicing dentistry and I started looking for a job.

Employment came easily since there weren't many physical therapists practicing at that time in Tennessee. I started working with the National Health Corporation, which was headquartered in Murfreesboro. Roy and I worked hard, long hours, yet since that was all we had done for many years in school, it seemed quite normal to us. In a couple of years, Roy established his own private practice, and a year later, I started my own private practice in physical therapy. Being a physical therapist in private practice was another new concept in the early 1980s. Roy still maintains a full-time dental practice today. I practiced for twenty-two years and grew my practice to include a home health agency in central Tennessee, numerous outpatient rehabilitation locations, and cardiac and workplace rehabilitation. With over two hundred employees at the time, Roy and I sold the practice and related businesses as managed care began making its entrance to the health care arena. For eight more years, I managed a large geographic area for the new company that now owned my practice. I was busy with three young children, supporting Roy's practice, and being involved in community activities. There was too little time for our marriage or the children, so in 1998 I chose a new direction for my life and retired from practice. What a great career I've experienced! Unknowingly, I was entering a new dimension of life—full-time manager of the children, house, and commercial real estate that was retained when my businesses were sold.

Heather was born in 1988, and we adopted her when she was one day old. Our friend—a physician we went to school with in Memphis who was in a family practice specializing in obstetrics—knew that we were interested in adopting a child. One Friday morning he called letting us know a child he knew of may be placed for adoption. It was a surprise for us when Heather's birth mother made this decision. We had been disappointed before when birth mothers had changed their minds. We had nothing in the way of baby equipment or clothing, and I wouldn't let my employees or friends give us anything, because in the state of Tennessee, the birth mother has fifteen days to change her mind with no questions asked. As a soon-to-be mother, I was guarding against disappointment. Everything worked out fine, though, and Heather was home to stay.

When Heather was six years old, Molly joined our family. We wanted a second child, and we had begun to actively work with the adoption network again. We were in the final stages of completing an adoption in China when the Department of Children's Services called Roy's office attempting to verify information on our initial application. We had been on the waiting list with the Department of Children's Services in Tennessee for ten years. Roy asked what the reason was for this unusual phone call. The social worker indicated that there might be a baby available in the near future. "Near" was an understatement! We met with the social worker the next day, and three days later we spent the afternoon with Molly and her foster parents. We took Molly and Heather to a hotel nearby, as was suggested to us by the social worker, and spent the afternoon together. The three of us fell in love with Molly by the time we returned her to her foster family that evening. The next morning, we met at the foster parents' house with the social worker to sign paperwork, and Molly came home with us.

Everyone was excited! We live in an established neighborhood, and in close proximity to our house there are nine adopted children. Knowing we were bringing a child home, the neighbors' children had waited and watched our house all day. As we were coming in the back door, they were ringing the front doorbell. The entire evening was spent with neighbors and their adopted children coming to our home. Family and friends arrived in the next few days. It was joyous! Molly is the youngest of our three children, but she was the second child we adopted.

Dylan is our middle child but the final one we adopted. He had just turned four years old when he joined our family. He came to us through our very first nanny, Kay. She worked for us until Heather started school. Kay had reared three biological sons as a single mother and was a professional at it. She came to visit us just a few months after we got Molly. She was concerned about her great-nephew, Dylan, and was seeking help. Dylan's living conditions were less than desirable, and Kay had been taking him to her house to care for him. Since we loved Kay so much and wanted to help her, we sought out legal advice for this particular situation.

Kay obtained temporary custody of Dylan, and we helped her care for him over the next few months as she attempted to work with her family members. Dylan's birth father was incarcerated at the time. Kay visited with him and his parents, then talked with extended family, trying to find a safe environment for Dylan. As time went on and no good solutions emerged, Kay came to us and asked if we would consider adopting Dylan. It was an easy decision for us. Roy and I felt that Dylan would not have a chance in life unless we stepped up to the plate and took responsibility for him. Our family of four grew to five.

Our Children's Special Needs Diagnoses

None of our children were identified as having special needs when we adopted them. Heather was always in trouble in her three-year-old class at preschool because she could not sit on her carpet square. Vanderbilt University Medical Center established her diagnosis of attention deficit hyperactivity disorder (ADHD), and when she entered school, we discovered her dyslexia. A lifetime of medications, followed by hours of special tutoring, marked Heather's life. Teaching her to read was such a challenge, and her learning disorder problems continue today. Although it was not an issue early in life, Heather deals with anxiety as an adult. She lives independently in North Carolina and maintains her life and a relationship with minimal assistance from either of us. She works full-time in the food industry.

Dylan arrived with a bucket of problems that we didn't anticipate. He had lived through much emotional trauma and neglect early in life. His abuse was basically emotional neglect but became physical over time. He had been left alone in an apartment for days at a time prior to the age of three. His psychologist diagnosed him early on with an attachment disorder—in other words, bonding with his parents had never happened. We innocently thought that with love and attention, Dylan would grow out of most of these issues. We also dealt with many food issues that were deeply rooted in Dylan's past. It has taken us twenty years of diligent work to teach him how to interpret and feel his emotions. We are seeing positive results from our years of work. Lying was one of his primary tactics for surviving in the world he grew up in. He was locked out of his mother's apartment during the day and left to wander the complex alone at an early age. His breakfast was at the local convenience store each morning. I still remember the day we were driving by that store and Dylan, at age eight or nine, turned to me and said, "The man that owns that store gave me my breakfast each day, didn't he?" My simple answer was, "Yes." As a mother, these stories from his past broke my heart. Dylan is bipolar and has ADHD, yet he is medically stable. After a stint in the Army, Dylan is now in college, studying wildlife sciences.

I thought it was cute when two-year-old Molly asked for a "shake milk" at the ice cream parlor instead of saying "milkshake." A year later, the preschool called and said they thought Molly might have ADHD. I knew how to get this medical evaluation, so we headed off to Vanderbilt University again. Molly received the ADHD diagnosis within two days, but what surprised me was that Molly was also diagnosed with an expressive and receptive functional language deficit disorder. Later, she was diagnosed with central auditory processing disorder (CAPD). She hears perfectly well, but her brain often scrambles the message, so she often doesn't hear the same words that others hear. She may hear a word that rhymes with the word that was just said.

We were exposed to a whole new dictionary with Molly. You can take a guess at what she meant by "washer wipers" on the car, and our car had two "trunks"—she just didn't learn that the front "trunk" was the hood. If she said something that we didn't understand or couldn't figure out and we chuckled over it, she became infuriated, and she could fly into a rage at age three or four. I actually thought that Roy and I invented the word "meltdown," because that is the only word to describe the frustration and tantrums Molly experienced so young in life.

Learning how to communicate with Molly, and teaching her how to communicate at school and with the world, was such a challenge for all of us. Ultimately, with a teacher's aide and some homebound instruction, Molly graduated with a regular high school diploma. Molly now lives in another state in a residential program for adults with learning disabilities. She lives and works with friends her own age and is extremely happy. Currently, we see no more meltdowns, but we still get new expressions. Recently, at Christmas, she said she was "second-thinking" herself when she meant "second-guessing." At this point, she too sees the humor in her made-up words.

Our Secret Parenting Weapons

When you read this book, you will learn two concepts or skills that we know have been essential to our marital and parenting success. No one taught them to us; we never read about them anywhere. You may use them to some degree already, but with a special needs family or difficult children, we feel they are critical. You will see them mentioned throughout the book. We call these parental secrets *pregaming*

Pregaming is simply talking through how an event should go ahead of time.

and *debriefing*. We haven't seen them discussed in any parenting literature over the years. Additionally, we have learned that honest and open communication between spouses is foundational to our success. Without communication, all is failure.

Pregaming. A pregame warm-up is similar to the sportscaster telling you how the ballgame is probably going to turn out even before you watch it. After the game, you generally say, "Bob sure did call it right tonight." Pregaming is simply talking through how an event should go ahead of time. It's advance planning on steroids. We spend a whole chapter on this subject, because our children were so disorganized, we had to learn how to apply structure to every aspect of their lives. As health care providers and business owners, Roy and I are extremely organized in our thinking and professional training. It took us a while to realize that our children did not have the same skills we possessed. It has been documented that children with ADHD lack executive-level organizational skills.

Debriefing. Reviewing the day, what worked and didn't, and how we could have done something better or different; discussing a physician visit; and sharing the details of the day are all debriefing. We did this every night in the privacy of our bedroom after the children went to sleep. We would share conversations the children had with us; review comments from physicians, teachers, and principals; and discuss behaviors that presented themselves during the day. We also reviewed our schedules, commitments, and possible future dilemmas. Problem-solving was included in this activity. It was also a safe time to share emotions with each other. Often, I was beating myself up emotionally about my parenting skills and I needed Roy's support.

Some nights the talks were long, but most nights Roy and I would end the debriefing with some humor—comments like, "Did Dylan really think that we would believe that story he told about Ms. Elliott? Does he think we are stupid?" We often thought our situation was so pitiful that we had to laugh. God apparently thought we needed to be humbled more or needed to stretch our brains and work harder. A critical part of the evening debrief is pregaming the next day. Trying to plan the day on the run at 7:00 a.m. never works in a busy family.

Communication

Throughout our professional training, continuing education, and work with outside professional consultants in our businesses, we realized that we have received a step up in knowing how to communicate. We don't underestimate this advantage in our lives, and this is one motivation for us to share our experiences with you. You are just as capable as we were of learning to communicate effectively. How many times have you been to a physician or dentist to discuss your health and had the conversation be so far above your head that you went home confused? Learning better communication skills helped us with patients and with our employees. Learning to ask questions was also critical.

There can be pitfalls with communication. Most people are not honest in their communications. They really don't want to say anything outright that will hurt an individual's feelings, but they lack the skills to communicate their own true feelings. For this reason, we make sarcastic and cutting comments to try and hint at our true meaning. These comments can feel like sticking a knife into someone and slowly giving it a quarter-turn. It hurts! As a physical therapist, I believe in being ruthlessly compassionate when I have to say something that might be painful. Employees give you a lot of experience with this technique.

We carry a lot of mental garbage around with us in an imaginary trash bag slung over our shoulders, stuffed with crumpled-up wads of paper for each time someone hurt our feelings and we never said anything to them. This bag stresses us out and weighs us down on a daily basis. You know these comments; you hear them daily. They start like this: "Last year on May 19, he told me . . ." or, "In the spring of 1982, she promised me . . ." or, "I'll never forget what he said to me . . ." You get the idea. We can be mean and cruel when we talk to the people we love the most. Please realize that your children hear your comments on a daily basis, and they will imitate your behavior.

Roy and I don't feel we could have been successful with our children without relying on each other and working together. Honest communication is a core principle between us. Our faith and our God have been active parts of this journey. Being committed to hard work has helped. For the most part, our children had a normal childhood, but it was dotted with psychologist appointments instead of Little League games. We have done the very best job that we feel we were capable of for our children, and now our goal is to continue helping them mature as adults. We are learning we will always be parents, no matter how long we live on this earth. No matter their age, children will always need our time and attention. Your family is unique, and you don't have to compare yourself to any other family you know. Believe in yourself! All of us are special and unique in God's eyes.

Our goal for our children was to let them thrive in a Christian home, prepare them to become good citizens and employees, and provide them a foundation for becoming excellent marriage partners. None of our children have married yet, but all three are Christians and are in college or working. Remember, it's progress, not perfection!

Although pregaming, debriefing, and honest communication are tools critical to our success, we also have five pillars that are the foundation of our marriage. The way trust, commitment, health, resilience, and optimism play out in your marriage can guide you and lead to success.

These are the choices we make:

- Choose Trust
- Choose Commitment
- Choose Health
- Choose Resilience
- Choose Optimism

CHAPTER 2

THE CHOICES WE MAKE

Part of the problem with the word "disabilities" is that it immediately suggests an inability to see or hear or walk or do other things that many of us take for granted. But what of people who can't feel? Or talk about their feelings? Or manage their feelings in constructive ways? What of people who aren't able to form close and strong relationships? And people who cannot find fulfillment in their lives, or those who have lost hope, who live in disappointment and bitterness and find in life no joy, no love? These, it seems to me, are the real disabilities.
—*Fred "Mr." Rogers*

ROY

Neither Margrey nor I ever went to the principal's office when we were in school, but we have made up for it as parents of Heather, Molly, and Dylan.

One day, my schedule was booked solid, and I was in the middle of a complicated procedure. As usual, I was engaged in the moment and as focused as a laser cutting through steel. I don't hear what people say unless they make eye contact, and at that time my eyes were on a tooth. I couldn't hear or see anything else around me.

"Margrey is on the phone, and she needs you now." My assistant's voice sounded like it was in a tunnel. She repeated her message. I slowed the drill until it stopped, excused myself from the treatment room, and took the call.

"Heather's principal called and needs to see us now," Margrey informed me. Her words were like the crack of gunfire. I couldn't ignore them.

"I've got patients all day."

"Heather's principal wants us to come to the school *now*."

"For what?"

"I don't know. But *now*." I could tell by Margrey's tone that we would be going to the school immediately.

After a few choice and inappropriate words about the situation, I got back into the zone, finished my patient's treatment, canceled the rest of the morning's patients "due to a family emergency," and headed home to pick up Margrey.

On the hour-long drive to Heather's school, I wondered what might have gone wrong out loud to myself. Margrey was silent. Heather was in eleventh grade at a private school for children with learning disabilities. Everything was progressing well. She was becoming a good advocate for herself, making friends, and discovering boys. She was thriving and happy.

> *"All I know, Roy, is that we are not driving to the morgue."*

Heather has a good heart. She's mischievous, forgetful, and scatterbrained at times, but she has never ventured into the waters of dangerous behavior. What could be going on that would get us called to the principal's office? I spent the whole drive thinking through every possible (and highly improbable) cause for the call. After miles of asking the windshield questions without receiving an answer, I asked Margrey, "Why are you not answering? Why are you not contributing?"

She looked out the passenger window at the rolling hills speeding by, and she said, "All I know, Roy, is that we are not driving to the morgue."

MARGREY

Another time, when Dylan was in third or fourth grade, I was in a class-room talking with Molly's teacher for a midyear review, as most mothers do on a regular basis, when there was a knock on the door. "Could I have a moment with you, Mrs. Thompson?"

I stepped across the hall into another classroom to meet with Dylan's teacher. We loved her. She had a staunch character and a bigger personality than her little body could contain. At that time, she didn't stand much taller than Dylan.

She said, "We had an incident with Dylan on the playground." The story spilled out of her mouth, and the more words she said, the more confused I became. I just didn't get it. The teacher asked the other boy involved in the incident to come into the hallway. He was much larger than Dylan, nearly as tall as me. Then she said, "I need you to go with Dylan to the principal's office."

As we walked down the hallway, I whispered to Dylan, "What's going on? What has happened?" When he told me, my hair could've curled without a perm.

ROY

After thirty years of marriage, I should know by now to listen to Mar-grey when she is telling me vital information. In 2007, Margrey had hinted—no, outright *told* me—that she believed Molly, then fourteen, was getting very interested in car keys. Using my keenly attuned audi-tory skills, I heard, but I did not listen, and I put this conversation out of my mind.

About four weeks later, a consultant was visiting my dental practice, observing my team at work and offering ideas on how to enhance our patient care. She and I sat down to go over her findings, and she inquired about my family and children; she knew I had three adopted children with special lives and needs.

Debbie, my office manager, entered the room; she made an apology for interrupting and whispered in my ear, "Your neighbor, Claudia, needs to speak to you. She said you should come to the phone *now!*" I've learned over time that "now" really does mean "immediately."

I was perturbed on the inside, but I excused myself from the meeting and took the call at Debbie's desk.

"Molly is driving your car around the block," Claudia said, wasting no time with pleasantries. "She's passed our house several times."

We live in a typical American neighborhood. I love it because I'm only twelve minutes from my office, even during rush hour. There is limited access in and out of the area, so little traffic interferes with kids' bicycle rides or middle-of-the-street conversations. Neighbors drive slowly. Our Neighborhood Watch group keeps a vigil at night and their fingers on the pulse of things during the day. We are close to our neighbors, and we pay attention to our children and our neighbors' children; we can even correct them without fear of our neighbors filing a lawsuit.

After first realizing the danger Molly might be in, my next thought was, *Which car is at home? Which car is about to be totaled?* Margrey drove a fairly new car; my car was ten years older than hers and was at the office. It wasn't hard to figure out that Molly was driving the new car!

We will get to the resolution of each of these special moments in a later chapter. For now, rest assured that everyone was okay and the situations were resolved. But how about you? How many times have you gotten "the call" in your situation? From where does your call come—your child's school, your caregiver's cell phone, a friend's parent, a Sunday school teacher in the hallway, a police officer at the front door, or a doctor in the emergency room?

You're doing well. Hear us loud and clear: you're doing well! You've made it this far despite the bumps and bruises. You wouldn't be reading this book if you didn't have an unwavering commitment to helping your child and supporting your spouse. That's worth celebrating!

Over the thirty years we've been rearing our children, we've learned a million lessons through a billion mistakes, many of which we made time and time again. Five of the most important lessons are outlined in the upcoming chapters. They are the five wheels on the car that have carried us in this journey (yes, in a special needs family there is a need for an extra wheel!). When one of these wheels gets lopsided, the driver can't keep the car on the road. If you read nothing else in this book, read about these five choices. If you apply none of the rest of this book, make these choices together with your spouse.

We know that even if you make these choices, your road will still be full of potholes, and from time to time a wheel will get out of alignment or shear off completely. However, if you *don't* make these basic choices, you will feel stranded on the side of the road, watching in horror as a Force-5 tornado bears down on you.

By their very nature, choices are difficult, and they never stop coming. In our work with patients, we occasionally have to refer them to a specialist. We have discovered that if we give a patient a list of two or three potential doctors to see, the patient is often frozen by indecision. When anyone fails to make a decision, in essence, they *are* making a decision—to continue on their present course of action (or inaction). By not making a choice, the patient makes a choice—to do nothing. However, when we give an enthusiastic recommendation of *one* specialist, the patient routinely follows through with the action, and their health improves. Confidently make choices and move forward in life.

In our marriage and joint parenting, we quickly realized that we faced thousands of choices. We limped along. Some evenings, we would flop onto the bed feeling battered by the day's decisions. Other evenings, we would've high-fived each other over the wisdom of our choices—if we hadn't been so bone-weary. As a rule, however, on the vast bulk of successful nights, we realized we had done exactly what we had observed in our patients: we had made a choice.

One night, Margrey and I found ourselves sitting at the kitchen table, considering our schedules. We were tired from the day's work, and the children were finally in bed and asleep. The kitchen was still a mess from dinner, the next day's backpacks needed to be packed, and communications to teachers needed to be written. Our energy levels were on empty. We sat in silence. The only noises in the kitchen came from the ticking clock and the icemaker in the refrigerator, dispensing its latest cubes. We were overcome by the enormity of the decisions we had to make daily in dealing with our children. We wanted more time for ourselves. We had to choose.

The choices we made that night were life-changing. I vividly remember telling Margrey that we were tougher, smarter, and more hard-working than the challenges that the children's uniqueness presented to us. I remember discussing how these three children were going to take some time to mature and develop, and I distinctly remember us deciding that *we* needed to mature also. We realized that, in our late thirties, we needed the

> *I vividly remember telling Margrey that we were tougher, smarter, and more hard-working than the challenges that the children's uniqueness presented to us.*

wisdom of a much older couple. Parenting these children was going to require life to be about them, not us. This was put-up-or-shut-up time.

As a husband, I remarked to Margrey that someday the children would be adults and move out of the house, and at that point, we would have more time for each other. It was a mutual and voluntary decision that we made together to preserve our marriage *and* get our children reared properly. That night, we began our rhythm of making all the best decisions possible, advocating with greater strength for our children, and becoming our own best allies. We didn't abandon our relationship or attention to each other; we simply realized that the children must take precedence for several years.

Are you stuck in your marriage or in the way you and your spouse are parenting? It's time to free yourself from those chains and move forward with purpose! Read these five commitments in the next chapters with the intent to make them. Wrestle with yourself first. Then make the decision with your spouse. Trust, commitment, health, resilience, and optimism, chosen together as a team, will help you overcome many obstacles in your marriage and parenting journey.

CHAPTER 3

CHOOSE TRUST

The best way to find out if you can trust somebody is to trust them.
—Ernest Hemingway

ROY

Imagine a red apple in the middle of a round kitchen table. Four people sit around the table.

The woman describes the apple, saying, "What a beautiful red specimen! Firm. Ripe."

The child pipes in. "Look at all those brown spots."

"Ew, gross. What is that wiggly thing?" cries the teenager.

The man says, "Hey, who took a bite? This was my snack for lunch."

Same apple; four perspectives. In your marriage, you will see hundreds of thousands of situations and incidents, and you will see them from different perspectives—same thing; two different points of view. There's a high probability you will *both* be right. There's also a probability you will both be *wrong*.

You're probably thinking, "Hey, guys, what about the times when one of us is absolutely right and the other is totally wrong?" Sure, there may be times when you are dealing with exact facts, like the dosage of Ritalin or the starting time of the spring recital; but for most of your disagreements, you are handling subjects that can be like that apple. From your perspective, you use your senses—and worse, your biases—to make judgments about the issue. You draw conclusions. Your educated and experienced mind begins to put your conclusions to work, deciding next steps and relationships to other issues. Meanwhile, your spouse has been at work too. They see it from their perspective. They see the worm and the bruises. Like you, they make judgments, draw conclusions, and decide on next steps.

Then you talk with your spouse. What is the average level of tension you experience during these oppositional moments? Friction? Sparks? Fireworks? Explosion? *Nuclear detonation?* If you are like us, most often one of us thinks we have the correct perspective. This can cause tension. *Deep trust* can ease that tension.

> *When your perspectives differ, you must trust that your spouse is making the best decision with the information they have at the time.*

The trust you share in your relationship is critical to your success in marriage and equally so in parenting. When your perspectives differ, you must trust that your spouse is making the best decision with the information they have at the time. You can't do that at all times unless you've developed a level of trust that is as deep as the taproot of your relationship.

How would you answer the following questions? Don't skim this list or pretend to be the perfect spouse as you answer. Consider each one, as well as your own past behavior.

I believe my spouse

- loves me unconditionally.
- is committed to me and to our marriage.
- knows my strengths and weaknesses.
- forgives me when I mess up.
- loves our child.
- deeply understands our child's special needs.

- will work tirelessly on behalf of our child.
- wants our child to be as healthy as possible.
- desires the best situation at all times for our child and our marriage.

Now consider the tougher part of this question. Change the questions around to consider how your spouse may view *your* attitude toward them. Does your spouse know deep in their heart that you love and trust them implicitly? Are you certain they feel you are aligned in your marriage and parenting views? To achieve long-term success, trust is critical. *Mutual* trust is paramount.

In conversations with couples we have talked with, most answer an emphatic "yes" to all of those statements; but the "yes" flies out the window when the desire to be right enters into a discussion or an argument.

Trusting your spouse means listening to them and responding to them. By doing so, you are expressing that trust. You are expressing the reality that you don't—and *can't*—see things from their perspective, yet you at least will hear their feelings and opinion nonjudgmentally. You are expressing that you trust their motives, their judgment, their instincts, and their record of past decisions and actions. When this trust is mutual, your marriage cannot be shaken, and your parenting will be a force to be reckoned with. Take a moment and stand in their shoes as they are talking to you. Can you feel their emotions? Can you see the problem they're discussing through their eyes?

Building Trust

The trust you crave already has a foundation. You already have enough evidence to trust your spouse! Allow us to present to the courtroom of your conscience the following data.

First, your spouse won your heart and affection and overwhelmed all others to the point that you planned and carried out a wedding, at which many friends and family members witnessed your vows to each other. Next, in the time before you had children, you and your spouse did things for each other—purchased gifts, prepared meals, mopped foreheads during illnesses, made love, paid rent, held hands at funerals, celebrated promotions, bought furniture, painted walls, and a thousand other things. Then you walked through pregnancy or adoption, nesting, birth, and the long nights of early parenthood. Finally, you've held each other as you've tried to come to grips with your children's special needs. There were many arguments along the way, but you've made it this far.

Imagine each event in your marriage as one mile of spaceflight. All of the moments you experience in just one year in marriage would reach to the moon and back! If you've been married more than ten years, you've traveled more miles than all of NASA's Apollo missions combined.

That's layers and layers of trust.

You can also *consciously* build trust. Here are four ways to accomplish this.

Make an Appreciation List. Each month, as a doctor, I start a team meeting at my dental office with this question: "What do you feel is the best thing that's happened in our practice since our last meeting?" We set the initial tone of our team meetings by focusing on the positive. Many counselors often prescribe this exercise in the first appointment of couples counseling. Most couples come into counseling with a list of grievances or criticisms; many counselors short-circuit this venting by asking each spouse to do this: "List out ten things you appreciate about your spouse." The task is difficult for some. It takes a little bit of goading to get the ink flowing for the first two or three items, but most individuals find that once started, the list can be finished easily. What if you created such a list about *your* spouse?

Develop a Gratitude Journal. Many life coaches suggest starting or ending the day by listing three simple things for which you are grateful. Purchase a notebook used just for this purpose. As you wind down before bed each night, write the date and at least three things for which you're thankful on that day. You can apply the same principle to your marriage: write down at least three things you're thankful about related to your spouse. Over the course of a year—even if you're very irregular with the exercise—you'll see a mountain of evidence related to how you can trust your spouse and how they can trust you. Some people prefer to set the tone of their day by doing this early in the morning. This starts the day by focusing on blessings. Whether you choose morning or evening, express in writing the things for which you are grateful. Go **BIG—Be In G**ratitude.

Keep Calendar Notes. If you're like Margrey, you use a calendar to keep track of your appointments and the activities of your children. Do you keep track of your spouse's schedule or how it is related to your children's activities? This requires very little change to your behavior. Just add your spouse's name to the appointments and occasions where they are involved or in charge. Then add an item to your schedule every time something happens—from a note left on a dashboard to a schedule change where your spouse helps you out of a jam to those privately heroic moments. Your schedule then becomes a record of faithfulness on which you can build trust.

Stay Alert and Aware. A record of trust does not necessarily mean keeping a file folder or a smartphone memo full of observations. As a matter of fact, the three previous suggestions don't work without this one. Become aware of what your spouse does and how they behave. Consciously recount how your spouse handled a situation. Hindsight is wonderful, and you can second-guess your spouse indefinitely, but in the chaos of the moment, when a child is having a meltdown at the grocery store or in the middle of the airport concourse, the best of us go into parenting survival mode. Always be aware and mindful, and no matter how minor, offer a word of thanks or praise. If you want to turbocharge your awareness, recount the story of something special your spouse did to someone at church, at a PTA meeting, or on an outing to the neighborhood pool. This tactic lets your spouse know you watch and admire them.

When Trust Is Broken

Many couples experience an "Apollo XIII" moment of broken trust in their journeys, when something explodes on the spacecraft and makes landing on the moon (deep trust) impossible. How do you recover trust when it's been broken? Trust is like a tower of blocks built with one single block at a time. When one block falls, many more may come tumbling down. It's a mess to clean up, and you have to start over, stacking a block at a time, but you become more skilled at stacking the blocks. Trust can be rebuilt faster with honest communication.

Soon after we were married, Margrey went through a period of months where her energy waned. Despite her training and experience as a physical therapist, it took several years before she received a diagnosis of lupus (specifically, systemic lupus erythematosus). In 1978, lupus research was thin, and there were many opinions about it. Her lupus would drain her of energy, like Superman in the presence of kryptonite (yes, she is my Superwoman). She soon learned the real definition of fatigue; she would come home after a long day at work and express regrets that she was tired. I would pick up the slack. To me that meant putting off any household duties and ordering in pizza. I would appear in the bedroom with dinner and find her propped up on pillows, struggling to stay awake, and my heart would ache for her. I even remember wishing I could do something to remove her lupus, not because it was a burden to me but simply to bring her relief.

On several occasions over the years, the phone would ring; a work associate would need her immediate help, and she would pop out of the bed like a six-year-old on Christmas morning, get dressed, and get to work solving the problem. After a few of these instances, I began to lose trust in her. Was she faking her fatigue? Was she using me? I developed a seed of resentment, because she could jump up for work associates but couldn't muster a tenth of the same energy for me.

I made the error of the apple. I wasn't seeing things from her perspective. She knew she was the only person who could solve the problem at hand. Margrey had a long history of excellent delegation, and if this associate was calling, her first instinct was to press the issue back on the associate to solve. If that didn't work, she carefully considered the consequences—problems for the patient, an unhappy physician, lost time, lost reputation, lost business opportunities—and made a calculated decision that she was the only one who could address the issue and that doing so right then was the best course of action. In those moments when my resentment peaked, I failed to remember the multitudes of times when she had built my trust in her decision-making.

After I had turned the volume of my resentment down enough to hear more than my own perspective, I brought it up with her. She was offended at first because she, like me, initially only saw the issue from her own perspective. Over time, we talked openly and honestly about her disease and the responsibilities of her private practice. We came to a mutual understanding and restored the trust that had been broken. Margrey and I have been blessed with very few breaks in trust; the times they have occurred are minimal. That may not be your story.

Broken trust is like water filling up a glass drop by drop. In the early stages of loss of trust, just like the drops in a glass, incidents are unnoticed and minor. As years pass, the glass fills. At some point, the water is bulging slightly above the top edge of the glass, and then a single extra drop makes it overflow. As trust is lost, the ache in your heart grows. It becomes easy then to misinterpret, with your prejudice and bias, the actions of your spouse. As you get pickier about the small stuff, trust diminishes, and at some point, the smallest or a seemingly insignificant thing totally breaks your trust. All sorts of anger and resentment spills over without limits. The water pouring from the glass makes a mess. A deep break in trust requires months of work to correct.

To restore the trust that may have cracked or shattered in your relationship, here are some suggestions. These activities may seem mundane or self-evident, but when trust is broken, it will tax your system. These aren't in any particular order, and not every one will apply to your relationship:

- Acknowledge that neither you nor your spouse is perfect.
- Remember that failure is not a sign of incompetence. We all fail. A common saying attributed to multiple sources is, "A person who never made a mistake never tried anything new."
- Tell the truth. When you lie—and you *will* lie—remember that a lie told is a horrible thing. No matter how small the lie is, it will

create a Grand Canyon between you and your spouse over time. A lie confessed and forgiven is like a scar, tender to the touch until time passes. Always tell the truth, and when you hear the truth, always forgive.

- When something goes wrong and you feel like you don't trust your spouse, hold your tongue and ask for clarity and understanding.
- Listen without thinking about your perspective.
- Take a deep breath before saying (not yelling) your response.
- When you see the strength in your spouse's positions and ideas, catalog this trust moment in your memory.
- If a debate is over verifiable facts, be gentle and merciful to each other when the data are revealed, no matter which one of you is correct. Realize that this minor fact will not change the world and that rubbing your correctness in your spouse's face will only cause resentment. Both of you, at some point, will be wrong, and you will want some latitude and forgiveness when you are the one who is mistaken.
- Remember, there are two sides to every argument.

The fact is that some of you are facing huge breaches in trust that you feel might be catastrophic to your relationship. You may be a wife married to a man who struggles to tell the truth. You may be a husband who has been cheated on. You may be married to someone that emotionally—or, God forbid, physically—hurts your children. If you are facing any of these or similarly heartbreaking trust issues, please seek the assistance of your pastor, a professional counselor, or local law enforcement.

MARGREY

My girlfriends are always surprised that I have the permission and freedom to handle our commercial real estate transactions. I tell them that my husband, Roy, trusts me. He tells me this, but he does more than that. He demonstrates that trust by applauding my decisions. He asks questions from time to time, but always with respect and a sense of curiosity, not superiority. The level of trust Roy places in me regarding these business deals is the same as he places in me in relation to our children. Real estate is a visible and tangible example to me every day of how trust has been fostered between us. It's so shocking that a business associate recently called Roy to clarify something. Roy laughed and said, "I really don't know the details about this aspect of our life. Margrey handles that; please call her." Sometimes even I forget just how deeply Roy trusts me! The associate laughed and replied, "I need to remember that Margrey has more business sense than you and I put together."

I feel esteemed, loved, and respected by Roy in this, as in so many areas of our relationship, because of the trust he's placed in me. When you have that much trust in your spouse, they will also trust you. If your spouse continues to question your actions after building that trust, perhaps the concerns are real and worth considering.

So . . . do you trust your spouse? Does your spouse trust you? Armed with the confidence that you and your spouse fully trust each other, focus on the commitment you made on your wedding day.

CHAPTER 4

CHOOSE COMMITMENT

*Desire is the key to motivation, but it's determination and
commitment to an unrelenting pursuit of your goal—a commitment
to excellence—that will engage you to attain the success you seek.*
—Mario Andretti

ROY

Margrey and I chose lifelong commitment—"till death do us part"—
before we walked down the aisle and years before we became parents. We
were both reared by families where it was understood that if you married,
you wore the rings forever, and if you had problems, you reconciled and
stayed together. The news media, daytime talk shows, TV dramas, movies,
novels, and our peers now make this type of decision appear old-fashioned
and unreasonable in light of the "statistics."

Don't believe everything you read on the internet! You hear these
figures as often as we do. Half of all marriages end in divorce; couples
raising special needs children are almost certain to divorce; 80 percent
or more of couples raising autistic children split up. We hear many people
quote these statistics, yet we could find no definitive research to support
divorce statistics for families like ours. The issues you and your spouse

struggle with are common to *all* couples. Some couples work through those issues and become stronger; other couples allow them to pile up like bricks, either creating a wall between husband and wife or allowing the weight of life to crush them. In the same way, your parenting of a special needs child can enrich and deepen your marriage, as opposed to overwhelming one or both of you.

You have no hope in the face of the challenges common to all marriages, or the additional pressures of raising a special needs child, unless you choose and stay determined to stay together no matter what. Open up every dictionary in the house and strike through the word *divorce* with a marker. Decide now to never again threaten—or even hint at—ending the marriage.

Recently, I picked up a magazine while Margrey was busy and read a short article titled "Marriage: To Stay or To Go." I was biased immediately, put off by the title, and I felt certain I would disagree, since my core value is commitment to marriage. The article, written by Andrew Aaron, was well written and presented both sides of leaving or staying. Laying aside divorces due to violence, addiction, or mental illness, he says, "Divorce does not deliver the sought-after happiness, though it may provide short-lived relief. Statistics support this by showing that second and third marriages result in divorce at a higher rate than first ones, also inferring that divorce does not teach ex-spouses to love any better."[1]

I agree with Mr. Aaron that staying married and working toward happiness is challenging and must involve the will of both parties to succeed. Divorce, in our opinion, is a cop-out, and we often read that others feel the same. However, commitment is a lot more than white-knuckling your way to a fiftieth-anniversary party. That's not a marriage; that's barely an existence. Choosing commitment means choosing the pain *and* the joy.

Commitment is *choosing* to make up after the fight. Choosing commitment enlists you as a firefighter; you run toward the fire when everyone

---

[1] Aaron, Andrew, "Marriage: To Stay or To Go?," *New England Monthly*, August 2016, 52.

else runs away. Our marriage has much love and much peace because we chose commitment, not because the road has been easy and lined with daffodils. Commitment will look different in your marriage than it does in ours.

Here are four ways we express commitment every day. As you read our list, think about your own marriage. What could be on your list? What are the most essential ways you express—or *want* to express—commitment to your spouse? What ways do you desire your spouse to demonstrate commitment to you?

MARGREY

Create a Safe Marriage. In my normal routine of performing physical therapy, I talk to my patients about so much more than just their physical rehabilitation. Topics come up; stories are told; we laugh and cry. I can't tell you how many times I've had a patient tell me something important and profound. I often follow up the patient's revelation, if they are married or in a relationship, by asking, "So what did your partner think about that?"

More times than not, a horrified look will appear on the patient's face, and she'll say, "I can't tell him that. Are you kidding me? You're not going to say anything to him, are you?"

I used to be shocked that patients kept their pain, physical dysfunction, or fears of living with their disability a secret from their spouses. They keep so much of their lives and feelings to themselves and don't share their emotions. If you can't tell your spouse about your feelings regarding your health and healing, how can you express your emotions about your marriage or your fears about your child? If you can't discuss, argue, and pray about your emotions and fears, how can you work together to raise your child?

Building a safe marriage requires the freedom to share anything about any topic without judgment from your spouse. When both of you are free to share anything without fear, the hard things become easier to say. It doesn't mean there won't be disagreements or even outright fights. One night, Roy came home to find one of the panes of glass in the back door broken out. Of course, he was concerned on several levels, and he questioned what had happened. At some point in what I thought was an exceptional parenting day, one of the children defiantly locked me out of the house. I had access to the garage and made the decision that the door must be open and I had to show this child that I had the wherewithal to get back in the house on my own. It is amazing how big of a mess a five-by-nine-inch untempered glass pane can make when a hammer collides with it! Roy just sort of shrugged and said supportively, "Good problem-solving"—and we moved on. This is the kind of commitment and trust a strong marriage needs. There were enough broken windowpanes over the years, for a variety of different reasons, that he finally put in plexiglass so the small pane could be easily removed to unlock the back door of the house.

Another evening, Roy arrived home and we sat down together on the couch. I looked at him and said, "I need to tell you something, and this needs to be one of those times you just say, 'Okay,' and we move on."

Roy looked at me, raised his eyebrows, and drew out his response. "Oh-kay?"

"While parking the big SUV, I sideswiped a telephone pole and ripped off the side mirror."

Roy squinted and responded, "Say *what?*"

The temperature jumped twenty degrees in the living room, but the heat evaporated quickly, because we had developed the habit of telling each other difficult things. There is another habit that is welded to it: not judging one another when something difficult is shared. In the years before this night, we had shared dozens of things harder than a minor car accident; and in the years since, we have shared many more difficult things. Sometimes judgment creeps into my heart, and I have to deal with it and then seek Roy's forgiveness. He has had to do the same. Sometimes our arguments grew heated because the issues were harder to resolve, but our desire for a safe marriage kept us on track.

Ironically, around this time, Roy had been teaching Heather how to drive, and he had commented on how close she was getting to mailboxes in the neighborhood. He had specifically mentioned she was going to take off the side mirror if she wasn't more aware of her surroundings! We laughed as he suggested I might need more driving instruction myself. Your marriage must have humor to get you through tough times.

Building a safe marriage allows you to practice total honesty. That means that you can eliminate lies, hopefully even so-called "little white lies." If you can tell your spouse *anything*, you will tell your spouse *everything*—in truth and without judgment.

It's also possible to show your ugly side when you're building a safe marriage. Your spouse sees your stretch marks, smells your morning breath, and trips over the shoes you can never seem to put away in the closet. A safe marriage allows you to feel open enough to show the unpleasant stuff that's inside. It's there anyway, and it needs to come out. There's no better place for that to happen than in a safe marriage. The Bible speaks about confessing your sins to one another. The purpose of this confession is so that each of you can be restored and made whole again. Mutual confession will build you up for the next day. Confess your shortcomings to your spouse. Lean on them for support and restoration, and be fully committed to each other.

ROY

Think the Best of Your Spouse at All Times. In my dental practice, as well as in parenting, I am asked a similar question almost every week. I've heard, "You mean you let Margrey make all those real estate decisions herself?" In parenting, it's, "Margrey didn't discuss that with you before she let Dylan do it?" I don't understand the motivation behind these questions, and it doesn't really matter that much. I know the truth: Margrey and I act as one unit. I trust her, and she trusts me. We have each other's backs.

We agreed early on as parents that I would be the primary caretaker of the children from 8:00 p.m. to 8:00 a.m. due to the inflexible nature of my schedule at the dental office. Margrey would be the primary caretaker during the day. Our work lives adapted well to this arrangement. During the day, I trust Margrey to make decisions and act without consulting me. I believe that she makes these choices based on the best information available at the time. Yes, this means that if we have better information hours or days later, we may change our minds and make a different decision.

I always back Margrey up, and she backs me up when it's my shift. We parent with a united front and commitment to each other. That doesn't mean we don't disagree. She always fills me in on the events and challenges of the day when we debrief in the sanctuary of our bedroom each night. I do the same in the morning if she slept through anything the night before. Because we think the best of each other, we start these discussions from a place of believing the other acts with integrity and wisdom and in the best interests of our children.

We start these discussions from a place of believing the other acts with integrity and wisdom and in the best interests of our children.

Because we create a safe environment within our marriage, we can talk about these matters with few explosions.

Thinking the best of each other takes practice. As health care practitioners, Margrey and I must be confident in our decisions. We run through a mental checklist to assess a condition and decide on the best treatment. We were trained to understand that confidence in our treatment would translate to our patients having confidence in us. In marriage, our first inclination might be to rattle off a list of all the better ways our spouse could've handled a situation. I know; I've been there. I've done it way too often and will probably do it again in the future. It's taken me a while to learn to hold my tongue and listen to Margrey before I respond. I also had to teach myself that Margrey's ninety-second summary of events may not include every detail, nuance, and precursor that led to the incident that needed a response. I've read Stephen R. Covey's *The 7 Habits of Highly Effective People*, and his fifth habit applies just as well at home as it does at the dental practice. He says, "Seek first to understand, then to be understood."[2] Thinking the best of your spouse means you understand the love of your life fully—in thoughts, words, deeds, and nonverbal communication—before you offer your opinion. If you're like me, you'll quickly learn that if you understand your spouse fully, you will keep your mouth shut more often. That's what commitment looks like in our eyes.

MARGREY

Extend Grace. *Grace* is a word with a thousand costumes. We watch Olympic gymnasts and ice skaters and marvel at their grace. Some families say grace before meals. If you're a fan of movies, no actress may be more aptly named than Grace Kelly. When we encourage you to extend grace to your spouse, we don't mean wear white gloves, bow to one another, and glide across the kitchen floor! The grace we are talking about is the *spiritual* definition of the word: offering a reward in place of condemnation.

Some use the words grace and mercy interchangeably, but there are significant differences between them. Mercy means *release from punishment*. Grace means *receiving a reward you don't deserve*. Mercy is *not giving* us what we *do* deserve; grace is *giving* us something we *do not* deserve.

Imagine being stopped for speeding on the interstate. The trooper approaches your car with his hand on the butt of his gun. You roll down your window. He says, "Do you know why I stopped you today?"

Your mouth is dryer than Arizona during a drought. "No, sir."

"I clocked you on my calibrated radar gun at ninety miles per hour in a seventy-miles-per-hour zone. License and registration, please."

---

[2] Stephen R. Covey, *The 7 Habits of Highly Effective People* (New York, Fireside Simon and Schuster, 1989, pg 235).

You hand everything over, and he returns to his car while your anti-perspirant fails. If the trooper returned and offered *mercy*, he would only give you an informal warning. Nothing would be noted on the computer. You wouldn't have to sign anything. You would be released from any punishment for your actions.

But if the trooper returned and offered *grace*, he would ask you to follow him to the state capitol, where you would receive a certificate of commendation from the joint legislature and a check for thousands of dollars.

So what does grace look like in marriage? First, it means that you don't ever seek to punish your spouse or intentionally make them look bad or wrong. You are not the judge, jury, and executioner in your relationship. It's not your responsibility to make sure your spouse knows what they did wrong and render a consequence tough enough that they will never forget it. Second, grace means you don't behave like a parent within the marriage; you are both of equal value. Third, grace means you are ready to forgive. One meaning of forgiveness is giving up one's right to punish another. Those who say, "Forgive and forget," are overlooking the fact that human nature is to remember. Sometimes we remember like the proverbial elephants. Forgiveness in marriage means letting offenses go in appropriate ways. Finally, grace means you always continue to give a gift to your spouse: the gift of yourself. Don't stop giving yourself to your spouse. This gift looks different each time you give it. It may be tears, a gentle touch on the shoulder, a lingering hug, sitting quietly together, a tickle fight, or an evening of lovemaking. Forgiving each other is easier if you always put the offense into perspective by looking at it side by side with other events in your life or with the troubles suffered by others near and far.

There will be days when you have to give grace a hundred times. Give early. Give often.

ROY

Always Show Respect. When Margrey and I first started working on this project, we thought of some of our favorite marriage stories. We both wrote out some thoughts, and then we shared with each other what we had written. I was blown away by what Margrey wrote. Here is a small part of it:

- Roy always puts my needs before his own, because he wants to. I never tested Roy's love on purpose, but he exhibits it daily.
- He always wants to kiss me goodbye before he leaves and say hello when he comes home.
- Sometimes he calls me when he has a break just to chat and hear my voice.
- He often asks me, "What can I do to help you?"
- I find notes on my bed when he leaves town, or a business card saying, "I love you," underneath the car's windshield wiper, or a surprise note in my suitcase when I leave town.

There were a dozen other things on her list, including some very specific memories I don't have the foggiest recollection of. I held the list like an archaeologist holds a thousand-year-old piece of intact pottery he's just uncovered. I felt honored and humbled; I felt seen and appreciated. But above all else, I felt *respected*. I smiled, because I have *always* felt respected—even on the toughest days, when a child is screaming and the police are ringing the doorbell.

I always strive to respect Margrey as well. The message seems to have gotten through, considering some of the things on her list—like these two items:

- When I want to talk and share my feelings (good and bad), Roy always stops and listens intently.
- Roy never says "no" to me about anything I sincerely want to do. He tells me I'm smart enough to make a good decision and talented enough to complete it.

Respect in marriage does not mean convening a meeting of your mutual admiration society and just gushing over each other. Respect is a core belief in each other. In your gut, you believe your spouse is intelligent, talented, wise, and ready to act in everyone's best interests. Respect is recognizing and using your spouse's strengths while minimizing the impact of their weaknesses.

Margrey and I have always had this respect for each other and have been smart enough to show it. We've met many couples, however, who struggle to feel respect for each other, let alone express it. If you're in that boat, may I challenge you to do what Margrey did? Think back on ways that you've felt loved over the years of your marriage. Early in our dating years, we tend to think our girlfriend or boyfriend is perfect. We think about them all day. We want to be with them all the time. We believe in them enough that we decide to have an exclusive relationship—to live with them or to marry them. Write down all the ways you've felt the love of your spouse. You'll be amazed at your list! Then share the list with your spouse. If you can, read it out loud to them.

The Don CeSar Hotel graces the sands of the west coast of Florida. Margrey and I attended a seminar at this resort when we were in our early thirties. We were poor and felt out of place there, but we fell in love with the historic and luxurious pink hotel. Since then, we have returned several times, more often for relaxation than for business. When you check in, you feel the euphoria of coming home again. You feel pampered and refreshed. The pool calls your name—and so do most of the employees. (I'm curious how they do that!)

Many years ago, we had both finished killer weeks at work and headed for Florida. We left on time for the flight, but airport traffic stressed us out. The flight was delayed and bumpy with turbulence. We finally made it to the Don and checked in for a four-day escape. Our clocks got turned around—nights literally became days. We would wake at noon and get some sun while reading by the pool, then return to our room, order room service, eat, and then go back to bed to nap. When midnight arrived, we'd turn on the television and watch movies until early morning, then nap again till midday. We threw the "Do Not Disturb" sign on the door, closed the curtains, and repeated this routine for several days. We lost ourselves in an oblivion of great books, television, food, sleep, and each other.

On Saturday, we heard music outside and pulled back the curtains to see a wedding in the courtyard below. Like other guests, we opened our window, watched the ceremony, and applauded the newlyweds. Newlyweds inspire me. They are like innocent children, who see only possibility. They challenge me to keep that newlywed feeling in my love for Margrey. After the bride threw the bouquet, we shut the window and curtains again and returned to our hibernation.

We've been to the Don multiple times over the decades, but something was special about that weekend. Time stopped. Margrey and I caught up. Locked up in that room and in each other's arms, we listened to each other's dreams and aspirations, and I felt an intimate bond between us. I know she did too. The trip rejuvenated our spirits. We felt heard and respected, and we were confident in our commitment to each other and our marriage.

How do you show your commitment to your spouse? You don't need a big pink hotel to do so. Just a few minutes together and a few words of support and encouragement every day can be enough. To have the strength to stay committed, though, you've got to take care of yourself. The next wise choice you should make is health. Your health is one of the best investments of your life. You are given an amazing body, but you only have one. How many times do you hear someone older and wiser say, "If I had known I was going to live this long, I would have taken better care of myself"? Don't gamble with your body. Choose health!

Interstitial Comment

Although much has been written suggesting that stress, grief, and other factors associated with parenting a child with disabilities results in high rates of marital discord, marital dissatisfaction, and divorce, this notion is poorly supported by research. Research demonstrates that parents of children with disabilities have marriages that exhibit the full range of function and dysfunction seen in the general population, most parents of children with disabilities have normal marriages, and the same things that predict healthy and unhealthy marriages in the general population also predict healthy and unhealthy marriages among parents of children with disabilities. A careful review of empirical studies of divorce rates of parents with and without disabilities suggests two reasonable possibilities: (1) There is no difference in divorce rates between parents of children with disabilities and parents of other children and most parents of children with disabilities do not divorce, or (2) there is a statistically significant but small increase in divorce rates among parents of children with disabilities. Even if the second possibility proves correct, it does not follow that increases in marital problems result from the children's disabilities. It is at least equally likely that family dysfunction increases risk for divorce and disabilities in children. While a great deal of research has attempted to demonstrate that children with disabilities are somehow harmful to their parents' marriages, very little attention has been paid to how bad marriages result in poor outcomes for children with disabilities.[3]

[3] Sosbey, Dick, "Marital Stability and Marital Satisfaction in Families of Children with Disabilities: Chicken or Egg?," *Developmental Disabilities Bulletin* 32, no. 1 (2004): 62–83.

CHAPTER 5

CHOOSE HEALTH

The greatest wealth is health.
—*Virgil*

ROY

If you've ever boarded an airplane, you have shown *trust* in the pilots. When the doors close and the wheels lift off the ground, you are *committed*. You've heard words like these: "In the event of cabin decompression, an oxygen mask will automatically appear in front of you. To start the flow of oxygen, pull the mask toward you. Place it firmly over your nose and mouth, secure the elastic band behind your head, and breathe normally. Although the bag does not inflate, oxygen is flowing to the mask. If you are traveling with a child or someone who requires assistance, secure your mask first and then assist the other person. Keep your mask on until a uniformed crew member advises you to remove it."

"Breathe normally"! That's like telling a woman in the middle of labor to "relax." Neither of us have ever been on an airplane during a flight emergency, and since our children are adopted, we've not experienced labor either. We can only imagine what it would be like for the engines to be grinding, luggage to be falling from the overhead bins, children crying and adults screaming, and the air crew trying to keep a calm demeanor, all while we are trying to "breathe normally."

While "breathe normally" sounds ludicrous, "put an oxygen mask on yourself before helping others" is as wise as if Solomon had said it himself. Putting the mask on yourself is an intentional act for the sake of yourself *and others*. Getting and staying healthy is also an intentional act for the sake of yourself and others. You can't help another breathe when you are unable to do it yourself.

To flourish in your life, you must be fully engaged. In *The Power of Full Engagement*, the premise of the authors, Jim Loehr and Tony Schwartz, is that you need to manage your energy, not your time, as the key to high performance and personal renewal. The focus of this book is physical energy, emotional energy, mental energy and spiritual energy.[4] This is never truer than when you're trying to keep your marriage strong while rearing a special needs child. When we are healthy every day, breaks in trust and lapses in commitment are more easily overcome. You and your spouse will struggle to handle all of the stress-inducing situations coming at you in life, work, and family if you aren't healthy and energetic in the above four areas plus with your romantic health.

- Physical health
- Emotional and mental health
- Spiritual health
- Romantic health

Physical Health

You've got to look at yourself as an athlete. Athletes eat, exercise, and sleep with purpose. For a world-class athlete, practice and conditioning make up 90 percent of waking hours. The game is only 10 percent of an

---

[4] Loehr, Jim and Schwartz, Tony, The Power of Full Engagement; 2005, The Free Press.

athlete's time and schedule. Rest is essential. For the parent of a special needs child, those percentages change. You have to be on your game 90 percent of your waking hours. What you do with the little remaining time you have to practice, condition, and rest (recover) makes all the difference.

Nutrition. Are you feeling the weight of maturity? In our twenties, we're invincible. We go at life fast and rarely think about our weight. At thirty, we are settling into life routines with kids, careers, and friends, and weight may begin to creep up on us. When I was in dental school, I could pull an all-nighter and manage fine the next day, but when I turned forty, I actually began to realize that I was aging and had to take better care of myself. It took me another ten years to actually begin to exercise regularly! Along the way, I read the book *Younger Next Year* by Chris Crowley and Henry S. Lodge and woke up to the necessity of maintaining my long-term health. I found passion in running and other sports, and I got back into shape. Margrey began walking regularly. Don't get me wrong—neither of us are elite athletes, but we are far from couch potatoes.

Hormones affect people as they age. Our metabolism slows over time. It takes fewer calories to sustain us as we age, but those calories need to be from healthy foods. We've all heard the messages before. Hundreds of authors tout their latest diet discoveries every year. Cable networks dedicate hundreds of hours a week to food and cooking. You can't drive far on most interstates without seeing both a billboard for a restaurant and a billboard for a weight loss clinic. Eating better shouldn't be a laborious daily chore nor break your bank account.

Keep things simple. You don't have to become a gourmet chef, serve a different meal every night, and plate your creations like works of art. Don't let the dozens of recipe videos on YouTube put pressure on you. Just get food to the table. Serve a meat (or other protein) and two vegetables. Find ten to twelve recipes that your family loves and rotate them. It makes shopping easier and less expensive, shortens your prep time, reduces stress, and helps you avoid the temptation of blowing off the meal prep in favor of drive-through fast food. It's important to eat in balance and eat together as a family as often as possible. Eating healthy isn't rocket science: Avoid fast-food temptations. Eat more vegetables and fruit. Eat fish and chicken more than red meat. Limit carbohydrates (bread, rice, and pasta). Avoid excessive desserts and sweets. Your plate should be half-filled with vegetables and fruit, a quarter with protein, and a quarter with a bread or other grain. Keep it simple!

Limit sugar. Don't forget, I'm a dentist. We reserved sweets for special occasions, and those were rare. There aren't many sweets in our house to begin with; what sweets we had were kept high in our bedroom closet, out of sight and reach. We found that the children got enough sweets during the hours they spent at school, at church, at social events, or on special holidays. We had a rule when the children were young that the sweets they got on one holiday would be thrown out prior to the next holiday—so whatever you got on Valentine's Day got thrown out at Easter if it had not been eaten. Same for Halloween; those treats got dumped on Thanksgiving. We limited soda too. Soda is absolutely the worst on your teeth and your weight, and it is quite expensive. Sports drinks and sweetened juices are chock full of sugar. Water and milk are better for the body, with far fewer calories.

Drink more water. If your body is craving fluids, you'll have trouble functioning. Don't consider your daily allotment of coffee and soda as liquids; only noncaffeinated drinks count. Here's a rule of thumb: if you're thirsty, your body is already on the verge of dehydration. Few people drink the recommended eight glasses of water daily. If you are exercising strenuously, you will need more. Nearly every one of us can do better in this category of hydration.

Limit alcohol. I love a glass of wine in the evening, but a bottle is a bit too much. Listen to your spouse and friends if they suggest you may be overconsuming. Seek professional assistance if this is a problem. Overconsumption of alcohol will wreck your health, your marriage, your career, and your entire life at some point.

Shop with purpose. Gather your top recipes and create a master shopping list for everything. Add breakfasts, lunches, healthy snacks, and staples to the list; then sort according to the arrangement of the aisles at your favorite grocery store. This way, you can buzz through without doubling back or crisscrossing, thus saving you time and frustration. If the experts are right, you will save money too, because you'll avoid impulse buying. Make copies of your master list and put them in your car so you've always got one handy. During the nightly debrief (more on this will follow), plan the dates of which dinners you will have at home. Assign the food options. Do this before you go shopping. Even if you don't plan and assign the meals, the organized list will help you shop and stay on budget. The goal is *simplicity*. As you get better at this simplicity, it takes hold and you learn to do it in your head and on the fly, but early on, write it all down. Don't skip over what we just said; I *still* keep lists. In the face of the distractions of work and parenting, lists are stress reducers; everyone is different, yet most of us need lists to stay on task.

Children value your time and attention more than anything you serve at the kitchen table.

We're not trying to make life bland. We know the power and pleasure of a well-planned and well-executed meal. But you have enough on your plate as it is! When your child looks back on these years, they will value and remember the time spent together around the table more than what was served. Children value your time and attention more than anything you serve at the kitchen table.

MARGREY

Exercise. Most of us know that burning calories doesn't have to burn a lot of brain cells or clock hours. As our bodies grow older, we must actively fight the effects of gravity and time. We aren't as active as we were in our twenties. Our bodies are busy breaking down. As a physical therapist, I've learned you need three things to maintain health: flexibility, aerobic exercise, and resistance training.

- **Stretch.** Have you ever pulled a forgotten, dried-up rubber band out of a desk drawer? Nonflexible and with dry rot, it doesn't stretch—it *breaks* when tension is put on it. When we don't keep our muscles and tendons flexible, they are headed toward this type of existence. Fifteen minutes a day stretching your arms, legs, and neck will help you maintain flexibility. While you watch TV, sit on the floor and stretch. Engage the children if they are still up. Start stretching exercises with your children when they are young, when they will see this as fun one-on-one playtime with you. At some point you will want to play on the floor with grandchildren! Make sure you maintain flexibility so you can get on the floor thirty years from today (and be able to get back up on your own).

- **Get your blood pumping.** If you briskly walk five times a week for thirty minutes, you are helping yourself live longer and healthier. As you improve, find some hills to hike. Park farther from the door of the supermarket. Take the stairs instead of the elevator. If you prefer, run, play basketball or racquetball, take a Zumba or Pilates class, or choose from a hundred other options. Don't be discouraged early on. Studies repeatedly show the benefits of consistent, lifelong exercise. Whatever you do and whenever you do it, get your heart rate up and sweat.

- **Pump some iron.** Weight lifting isn't just for the Arnold Schwarzeneggers of the world. Using resistance bands or hand weights is a simple way for men and women to ward off osteoporosis. If you're lucky enough and have the luxury to do so, enlist the assistance of a trainer. Challenge a friend to join you and remove the intimidation factor of a gym, where you will have access to weight machines. Many communities have recreational centers, and they invite the public to join at minimal or no fees. These public facilities where you can exercise and use weights often have group classes, and you can socialize with new friends.

There are so many other benefits to exercise. Roy and I both work out with friends. It's a great time to connect with others. We enjoy the release of endorphins—God's pain medicine—generated by the body. Exercise is one of the most consistent forms of stress relief, and we know you need that! Whatever you do, start some form of exercise today; and as you are always warned, make sure you are healthy enough to exercise. Check with your physician first and start slowly. Don't go out and get hurt. You can't serve your family very well if you are laid up in bed! Another overlooked aspect of exercise is that it can be incorporated as a family event. Your children will see you exercising, and it will rub off on them. Good health is a family affair.

Sleep. As an individual with lupus, I really understand and live the words *fatigued* and *tired*. When my disease was active, all I wanted to do was sleep. Sleep is super important in everyone's life, even if you have no medical dilemmas. You'll get more done in fewer hours with proper sleep than you'll accomplish in more time while exhausted. With few exceptions, the parents of special needs children we meet are all exhausted, and they struggle to get enough sleep. If you fall into that category, here are some pointers to help you sleep better and more soundly:

With few exceptions, the parents of special needs children we meet are all exhausted, and they struggle to get enough sleep.

- **Get your children on a sleep schedule.** Set a bedtime for all children, and have a routine. Just as you need regular routines to prep your mind and body for rest, so do your children. Don't expect to be roughhousing at 8:30 in the evening and then ask the kids to jump in bed to sleep at 8:45. Be realistic. After homework and dinner, limit their screen time (TV, texting, social media, video games, and computer time). Get them moving to take their baths, brush their teeth, and get ready for reading time. Get them in bed thirty minutes prior to lights out. Don't violate their nighttime schedule to pursue your own agenda! The better they sleep, the more likely they will be to hop out of bed on time the next day—and the more likely you will be to get to bed on time too.

- **Relax before you sleep.** When doctors recommend purposeful relaxation, they're not talking about a couple of brews and a baseball game on TV. That type of relaxation has its place, but sleep specialists recommend breathing deeply for a minute, stretching tired muscles, and listening to whatever music soothes you. Many people enjoy a few minutes of reading prior to turning out the lights.

- **Turn out the lights.** Most of us sleep best when it is fully dark. If you can't handle a total blackout, use a soft nightlight.

- **Place your clock facing away from you.** Roy noticed several years ago that he was waking up multiple times a night and glancing at the clock. He wasn't sure if he was worrying about oversleeping or just curious about how much more sleep time remained. He always said he would go back to sleep immediately and thought no more about it. Ultimately, he realized this wasn't healthy (or normal), so he began to block the clock from view. The room was darker; he quit waking in the night, and he slept more soundly.

- **Avoid excessive napping.** Sometimes you do need a power nap of fifteen minutes or so. This typically will not affect your nighttime sleep. However, if you jump in bed and find yourself waking up two hours later, you will not sleep as well that night. Ten hours of sleep a day is not necessarily better than the recommended eight hours. If you find sleep doesn't come easily, evaluate if you are sleeping too much during the day.

- **Make it cold.** Many people stay asleep better in a cold space. We sleep with a ceiling fan running above our heads all year round. The hum of the fan and waft of air just seem to relax us more.

- **Cut out the screens.** Just like your children, you shouldn't look at a television, smartphone, laptop, or tablet for at least an hour before going to bed. Several years ago, Roy pledged to get away from the computer by 10:00 p.m. That didn't work. It took him a month to realize that if he was going to bed at 10:30, thirty minutes was not enough downtime from the stimulation created by Facebook, emails, and other business created by the computer. Now he tries to turn the screens off by 8:00 p.m. so he can be asleep by 9:00 p.m. Generally, don't try to go to sleep watching television or watch a shoot-and-kill dramatic movie late at night. The light from the screen tells your brain that the sun is coming up, and the content of the programming will have you hot-wired for action.

- **Go to bed at the same time every night.** Like your children, your body craves routine. We know your life is anything but! A consistent bedtime tells your brain and body to rest. Otherwise, your body is trying to stay alert and do some work.

- **Work out bedtime agreements with your spouse.** Since Roy is an early-morning runner, he needs to go to bed earlier than me. This can and has been a source of friction for us, as our bedtime routines differ. Unlike what was said just two paragraphs earlier, he can watch an action-packed television program and fall asleep ten minutes later. He can read two paragraphs of a book and immediately go to sleep or he can exercise at 9:30 p.m., shower, and be asleep within minutes. Most people are not so fortunate. I come home totally exhausted and fall into bed but then read for an hour or more before being sleepy. I like to use an electric blanket year-round to minimize the joint pain from my lupus. Roy sleeps with minimal cover and hasn't plugged in his electric blanket for years. It is not fair, though, for Roy to have the TV screaming drama and expect me to watch it and fall asleep as easily as he does, nor is it fair for me to use the overhead light for reading until midnight while he's sleeping on the other side of the bed. Nighttime agreements help solve these differences. Over time we've agreed to lights out around 9:00 p.m. I now uses a digital e-reader or a small book light when I want to read late into the night. There is no banging around the bedroom when the other is asleep, and we have dual controls on the electric blanket. You will find your own compromises, but respect is the basic tenet of these agreements.

Emotional and Mental Health

In a later chapter, we will go into much more detail about how important it is for you and your spouse to receive the counseling you each need. Each of us carries baggage—good and bad—in our lives. In the past, therapy has carried the stigma that something is wrong with the person lying on the couch. A skilled psychologist will help you be more effective and healthier in your life.

Some couples receive premarital counseling. Unfortunately, at that time you are starry-eyed and hopeful, and you can only see one or two steps ahead. Now that the reality of raising special needs children is more immediate to you, marital counseling may be your lifeline. It will do wonders to align your vision around your marriage. Counseling doesn't need to entail a lifetime of private and sometimes out-of-pocket expense. Many religious organizations may offer counseling for reduced fees or no fee. Many communities also have programs at low or no cost. Check out your options, and don't dismiss counseling as something that is expensive or unnecessary.

Have you ever heard the phrase "self-care"? In addition to counseling, we need to take care of our minds and hearts on our own. In the same way that your medical doctor can't exercise for you, your counselor can't complete the emotional self-care you must do on your own; and as we noted above, self-care doesn't have to be complicated or time-consuming. Take time by yourself in the middle of the day to breathe deeply for two minutes. Read a couple of paragraphs from a devotional or a book each day. Call a friend often and talk (texting isn't the same). Listen to music, sing in the shower, or do something that makes you smile. Laugh often, and by all means, learn to laugh at yourself. Learn to laugh with your spouse. Don't miss these last two sentences. You must learn to laugh, or too often you may cry.

Spiritual Health

Roy and I are spiritual beings. We believe in God; we believe that the Bible is true and that Jesus Christ is God's only son who is fully God and fully man, and that He came to Earth to be the substitute for the punishment we deserve for the bad things we've done, are doing today, and will do tomorrow. We believe that His crucifixion, death, burial, resurrection, and ascension are historical facts and that they conquered death for those who believe.

These core beliefs inform our work, our home, and our relationships. We don't know where we'd be without God's role in our lives. You may believe something different. Our goal is to give you a full view into what has worked for us, and we know our faith is a great source of our peace and success. No matter where you stand on spiritual matters, let us offer three concepts for you to consider.

Prayer. A Duke University study called the MANTRA project showed in 2001 that prayer of differing types may help outcomes after surgery.[5] There are hundreds of studies on the efficacy of prayer, and scientifically the reports show mixed outcomes. Yet when you focus on positive outcomes, we feel this cannot work negatively in your life. When was the last time you prayed for your spouse and children? God hears your prayers and your cries for help. The Bible even tells us that Jesus's job right now is to sit at God's right ear and pray for us.

---

[5] Mitchell W.Krucoff, MD, Suzanne W.Crater, RN, ANP-C, Cindy L.Green, PhD, Arthur C.Maas, MD, Jon E.Seskevich, RN, James D.Lane, PhD, Karen A.Loeffler, Kenneth Morris MD, Thomas M.Bashore MD, Harold G.Koenig MD, Integrative noetic therapies as adjuncts to percutaneous intervention during unstable coronary syndromes: Monitoring and Actualization of Noetic Training (MANTRA), American Heart Journal, Volume 142, Issue 5, November 2001, Pages 760–769.

Sentence prayers, or "prayer darts," are great. Cry out to Him all day every day. God knows your needs better than you do. He knows your heart and loves you with a powerful affection too great for words. He doesn't need to hear all of the specifics; however, specifics have their place. They help us to order our thoughts. The apostle Paul, who wrote much of the New Testament, wrote out his specific prayers at the beginning of each of his letters. Pray continuously to God. Long ago, as a physical therapist, I invited God to be part of my daily self-talk and my conscious thoughts. There were so many decisions to make about patients and staff that my self-talk with God became a continuous prayer all day long. I always have the opportunity to talk openly to the Father, a parent who loves me so much and supports me in all my concerns, thoughts, and anxieties.

Consider praying aloud together as a couple. If you've never tried it or haven't prayed in public yourself, this can feel scary and even weird. Roy and I prayed in our home at meals throughout our marriage. We prayed when our children had friends over for dinner so that our children were always comfortable with prayer. We pray at family gatherings, but for years we never prayed aloud together in private for some reason. Several years ago, however, a friend encouraged us to make it a nightly habit to pray aloud together. We took her challenge, and we added prayer to our nightly debrief. We've discovered, much later than we should have, that openly praying at bedtime is liberating and very intimate. Praying at night for our blessings ends each day successfully, just as writing down our list of what we're grateful for in the morning starts our day off right. We offer thanks for our blessings; we pray for our children's continuing maturity and health and for our friends who are struggling; and we lift up prayers for each other's health, well-being, safety, and success. Roy and I are both thankful we do it now, and we regret not having started years earlier. Praying together allows you to hear the depth and breadth of your spouse's joy and hurt, and it allows you to express your own and be heard.

Meditation. Similar to prayer, meditation offers you a time of quiet and peace. However much time you dedicate to meditation, you can focus on your life, your blessings, and your needs. This time of quiet allows your subconscious to work out whatever problems and frustrations you may be facing. Ideas bubble up; inspiration comes. You can look at the previous day and see how you could have done better or been better. Meditation is a time for introspection; it is not a time to analyze how your spouse could be better. It can be a time to focus on the strengths of your children and how far they have come. It may be a time for you to appreciate nature and a world that is bigger than us as individuals. Meditation offers the opportunity to

- reduce stress,
- increase self-awareness,
- embrace a healthier lifestyle,
- increase concentration,
- increase acceptance,
- slow the aging process,
- benefit cardiovascular and immune systems,
- increase happiness, and
- improve your social life.

Whether you engage in prayer, meditation or both, this time alone brings mindfulness to your life and allows you to center yourself. You must stay healthy for your family. Use every tool available to improve the odds of you staying healthy.

> *You must stay healthy for your family. Use every tool available to improve the odds of you staying healthy.*

Church Community. Being a part of a religious or spiritual community is a lifeline. You will have traveling companions for every step of the road of life. You will discover that you're not alone. The teaching you receive will contribute to your psychological health. You will laugh and cry, which have great benefits. More than anything, you will have a support system around you. Your church family can become a safe haven for you and your family.

No church is perfect. If you feel looked down on or marginalized, speak to the leadership; if it continues, change churches. More and more churches are developing programs to help couples and families with special needs children.

ROY

Romantic Health

Many years ago, Margrey and I had a soul-searching conversation and came to the conclusion that with the complex issues facing our children, we would not be able to do leisure activities as often as we had previously anticipated. We mutually decided we had to hunker down and raise these children together. We both saw the reality of our lives and knew we would have to put our romantic life into the schedule like every other activity. We also were mature enough to realize that once the children were more self-sufficient, we would have time to spend with each other.

Instead of roses and candles during those years, we found romance where we could. Our romance came from the joys of successful parenting at times. It came from cleaning the house, from getting the garden weeded, or from cleaning out the attic or garage together. We live across the street from Middle Tennessee State University (MTSU), where we have access to twenty thousand students looking for part-time employment. This allows us the opportunity to find a babysitter who can help us to have a date night. Thankfully, my travels with the American Dental Association allowed us an occasional romantic getaway while still accomplishing business at the same time. The romanticism of our marriage never was extinguished; it just couldn't burn quite as brightly when three highly energetic children were running around the house. Now, with the children out of the house, the benefits are sweeter than we could have imagined.

Acknowledging the reality of your existence doesn't mean you become automatons or robots. It doesn't mean you put your sex drive in the attic. We will discuss five ways to change your perspective and expectations.

MARGREY

Date Each Other. Before you were married, I bet you dated more than once a week. Concerts, dinner, movies, parties—why do we stop when we get married? Raising a special needs child is time-consuming, stressful, and expensive. Dating doesn't have to mean five-star restaurants and tickets to a Broadway show; sometimes it's locking the bedroom door early and eating delivery pizza by candlelight in the middle of the bed. Find a way each week to spend some one-on-one time, even if you can only go grocery shopping together. At one point, Roy and I would sit on the couch when he got home and visit with each other for about fifteen minutes before we had dinner. Children were not allowed to interrupt us as we shared our day. I believe this carried weight with the children in their earliest years, to see us together as a unit and understand that our private time was important.

Like every other thing of value, you must be intentional about dating. When you debrief and pregame every night, don't neglect to add your dates to the calendar and budget. Within a few weeks, you'll feel closer and be more aligned.

Roy's team at the office often gives him a hard time because our favorite restaurant is Applebee's. They say we're not romantic! The food is good, it's close to our house, and we've just about memorized the menu. Recently we discovered another venue for evening meals: On one of our afternoon walks, we happened upon Callie's Café, one of MTSU's dining halls. For a small price, we get protein, vegetables, salad, the drink of our choice, dessert, and a chance to pretend we are still college students.

Our date night is simple, close, and convenient. A date doesn't have to be a hundred-dollar meal!

One of our favorite anniversaries occurred during a weeknight, when we had come home from work prepared for our raucous dinnertime meal. The children were between the ages of six and twelve years old. We had no anniversary plans, just the evening routine of homework, baths, and bedtime. A romantic note in a Hallmark card would be the extent of our celebration. Unbeknownst to us, however, the children, with the help of the babysitter, had set up a table and chairs in our bedroom, complete with china and crystal. The children asked us to sit, served us a meal prepared by the sitter, and left us alone in our bedroom. The two of us had a quiet anniversary dinner. Times like that made us proud that something was going well in our family. These are the times you must celebrate more than just an anniversary.

> *Times like that made us proud that something was going well in our family. These are the times you must celebrate more than just an anniversary.*

Get Away. Imagine eating only healthy snacks and never a substantial meal. Every couple needs long periods of time together. Getting away helps your physical and psychological health; your stress level decreases, your mind decompresses, and you can talk on a different, deeper level.

Finding childcare can be the biggest obstacle to getting away. You'll need to plan to find someone to care for your special needs child. Begin discussing it early. You might want to enlist the help of another family member you trust, and you, in turn, can watch *their* child. Once you have a family member or friend who can help, make sure you set out clear expectations and boundaries. Prepare your child in advance by letting them grow more comfortable with your trusted person; then, when you get away, let go. The goal is for your friends or family to simply keep your child safe.

We recommend getting away at least once a year. And "getting away" can mean sending your child to visit a relative, which will be fun for them as well, so you can be at your home alone. The goal, though, is to relax and spend time together, not catch up on projects at the house. The pitfall of just staying home is that the yard, dishes, laundry, and email are all there to distract you, so if it fits your style and budget, try to leave the house. The first couple of times you get away, just sleep and reconnect. Rest your bodies and souls and celebrate your marriage. Eventually, you'll get into a rhythm that will allow you to talk about your dreams and plan the future. Know this: Sometimes your getaway will give you just enough time to breed conflict. That's okay! Just work together and work through it.

Schedule Time for Sex. When your schedule is full of work, family, doctor's appointments, paying bills, and other obligations, sexual intimacy can get left behind. This can be frustrating for both of you. Be as intentional about intimacy as you are about dating. Next Thursday, are you both free over lunch? Has your child been invited to a birthday party next month? You get the idea: Find the time where you can. Schedule it like an appointment, as boring and nonspontaneous as that sounds. We promise it won't be!

Adjust your expectations for making love too. Many couples believe if sex is rare, the times when they *do* connect need to be full of fireworks. There are as many kinds of lovemaking as there are kinds of restaurants. Tonight might be a fast-food burger, and next week may be king salmon with all the trimmings. Both are delicious and have their place. Connecting and enjoying each other's bodies is the essential matter.

Touch Often. The first of our five senses to develop is touch. Don't neglect to touch each other. When couples are in the early days of their relationships, they can't seem to stop touching each other. Why does this change as we grow older? Get back in the habit of touching, hugging, and kissing as often as you can. It doesn't matter how; give each other high fives or a fist bump as you pass in the house. Hold hands as much as possible. Rub each other's tired muscles. If you're within an arm's length of each other, make the effort to touch. Do this visibly and in front of the children. Displaying affection openly yet appropriately teaches children that love comes in many forms and is as natural as breathing. At the same time, remember to touch your children on a daily basis. This will become naturally engraved in their minds, and later, when they are in a relationship, they will remember the comfort of touch.

ROY

Build Protective Walls. Charleston, South Carolina is a breathtaking city full of history, art, cuisine, and architecture. There is a famous 250-year-old wall standing along its lower shores known as the Battery. This wall has endured countless storms, tides, and even the Civil War. Beautiful mansions stand behind the Battery facing the ocean. The wall protects them all.

Your marriage is like one of the homes along the Battery. It needs walls of protection from outside storms. In 1989, Hurricane Hugo changed the landscape of the Battery. Hugo's Category 4 power and 140-mile-per-hour winds slammed the coast, causing billions of dollars of damage to the southeastern United States. While the Battery was hit hard, it still performed its duty. The homes there sustained less damage than homes that were unprotected. The Battery itself was not destroyed, but the storm weakened it. Like Charleston, your marriage can withstand the worst storms if you have the proper defenses.

Do you have walls protecting your marriage? We set boundaries and expectations for our children; why are we so reticent to do the same for our marriages? While we were writing this book, the news media was abundantly covering sexual scandals in both Hollywood and Washington, DC. In this day of heightened attention to sexual misconduct, it is wise to set boundaries and not cross them.

The greatest protection we have for our marriage is open and honest communication, along with our trust and commitment to each other. Years ago, Margrey was at a physical therapy meeting in Florida. Margrey told me that after one meeting, people were sitting around the pool, relaxing and enjoying the weather. A colleague fifteen years older than her casually asked her to come to his room. She declined his offer and called me that night, nearly in tears, to share the incident with me. Several months later, Margrey received a letter of apology from this colleague, and she continued a healthy business relationship with him over the years. Margrey and I have always found sanctuary at home and in each other because we enjoy each other's company. Peace comes from being with your spouse. In addition, any marriage expert will remind you to stay away from trashy novels, pornography, having your closest friend be of the opposite sex, and finding pleasure in the company of others more than with your spouse.

We feel like after reading this chapter, you may need oxygen. Children like yours need your full energy. A life like yours needs fully engaged spouses and parents. Getting healthier in any area takes time and incremental work. If you need to lose weight, you're not going to drop thirty pounds tonight; and in much the same way, you can't implement every suggestion we've offered in a few days or even weeks. You have to breathe. Start small, and add another healthy suggestion every few weeks. Don't give up! Your spouse and your children need you. You will be healthier and be able to do more, and you'll be more emotionally connected, as you do. As you get healthier, you can better withstand the storms to come. This strength will improve your resilience. There will be setbacks, and you must be able to bounce back fast. Your marriage and children will count on your strength.

So put the oxygen mask on yourself and try to breathe normally.

CHAPTER 6

CHOOSE RESILIENCE

A good half of the art of living is resilience.
—Alain de Botto

ROY

When was the last time you looked up a word online instead of moving forward with only your understanding of its definition? Take *resilience*, the key word for this chapter. Some might think the word means to roll over life like an all-powerful bulldozer, crushing every obstacle and running through every trial with ease. Some might liken resilience in a human being to not being fazed by anything that happens. No matter what events transpire, a resilient person shrugs, says, "Oh, well," and moves on.

But what *does* resilience mean? At its root, *resilience* conjures up trouble, misfortune, trials, hard times, and stress. These stressors make us stronger. Just as a muscle must be flexed to grow stronger, our trials in life force us to grow and become more resilient. Resilience does not include perfection, ease, or being a Superman in its definition. Resilience is the ability to recover and repair. Resilience looks like a farmhouse that needs new windows and a roof but still stands years after a devastating tornado. Resilience's foundation is health.

You may not feel resilient right now, but you are. How old is your special needs child? Reflect for just a few seconds on some of the challenges you've endured. You're still standing! How long have you been married? What are three fights you've struggled through? You're still moving! You're reading this book and searching for answers or deepening your resolve to see this process through. Whether you are reading to strengthen your marriage or to improve your outlook and attitude toward raising your children, you are still searching and growing. This is resilience. We said our mantra toward our children's growth is "progress, not perfection"; so too is our mantra toward life.

You have been resilient, and this resilience is based in health. If you aren't healthy physically, mentally, and spiritually, your ability to survive the storms of marriage and of raising special needs children will suffer. You must take care of yourself so that you can be a partner in rearing children *and* a partner in marriage. Resilience will create reserves of energy, and success depends on your full energy and engagement. Your family deserves nothing less. Your engagement and

> ### You may not feel resilient right now, but you are.

partnership should be 100 percent. If your goal is that you and your spouse each contribute 50 percent, when one of you falls short, there will be no meeting in the middle. There will be a gap between the two of you. Success requires your full engagement in all aspects of this venture.

To move into the future, to survive for the duration of your marriage, you will need to choose resilience. You will need to say something to yourself like Margrey says aloud in the car some days: "If Roy isn't here with me anymore, I will have another twenty years of being a mom to these three kids. I have a plan; I'm praying; I will be resilient." Does that sound morbid to you? Rid yourself of that thinking! This is the attitude that will get you through the tough times ahead. This goes back to giving and committing 100 percent. In the unfortunate event that one of you must raise these children alone, you will need to give 100 percent to succeed.

Enduring Loss: Resilience of Spirit

We'll say many times that as part of your marriage journey as parents of a special needs child, you will need to adjust the goals you have for your child and your expectations as a parent. You will still be button-popping proud of them, but your joy in their accomplishments will come from a different place than that of parents of typical children and will be measured according to a completely different standard, as different as Fahrenheit and Celsius. Recalibrating your hopes and dreams for your child may shove you into the grieving process. You will also have to let go of, or at least delay, some perfectionistic dreams of your marriage and the life you've envisioned, because vacations won't be the same, and the empty nest years may be delayed—or may never come.

The grief process for you isn't a one-time event. You will go through the cycle many times, with every developmental phase your child enters. You can't look at grief as a checklist; you must look at it as a journey. When Swiss psychiatrist Elisabeth Kübler-Ross outlined the five stages of grief in her 1969 book, On Death and Dying, she postulated that they were a predictable progression from one to another. However, the five stages—denial, anger, bargaining, depression, and acceptance—are not a linear stream of emotions.[6] You don't move from a beginning point to an ending point in the grief process like you would driving I-40 from Memphis to Knoxville. Thirty-six years after writing her groundbreaking book, she wrote of regretting her original ideas because so many interpreted her work as a formula, not as a collection of observations. You don't experience one stage, complete it, and then move on to the next one. There isn't a standard length of time for your duration in one stage. Each parent stays in the grief process for a different length of time. No two experiences are the same. You will spend the majority of your time in the bittersweet meadow of acceptance, but your child lives on, and you will be reminded often of your dreams.

---

[6] Kübler-Ross, Elisabeth, On Death and Dying, 1969, Scribner, New York.

Instead of looking at grief as a process, look at it as a dense forest through which you're making great strides and progress. Every few steps, you'll come across a tree. Sometimes that tree will be an oak (acceptance); other times you will rub the bark of a pine (anger) or trip over the roots of a maple (denial). With every tree passed, you will feel the skinned knee, splintered finger, or twisted ankle of a person in process. Your grief journey will take you past many different types of trees. You'll wonder sometimes if you're going in circles, but you must keep moving toward the soft light filtering through the trees at the edge of the forest. A meadow and brook await you there. With each tree encountered, you will stand up straight, dust yourself off, and remind yourself of the true nature of resilience.

Finding Care: Resilience of Soul

Choosing the professionals who will walk with you on your marriage and parenting journey is one of the most important decisions you'll make. We will go into great detail about this issue in a later chapter. But for now, let us address how your counselors and therapists help you stay resilient.

The earlier you enlist the right professional help, the better off you will be later. You can easily find a calculator on the internet that shows how saving $2,500 per year in an IRA (just over $200 per month) beginning at age eighteen and continuing for twenty-five years will yield over a million dollars by age sixty-five. Compounding interest (in this case around 8 percent) will pay huge dividends, and they will add up over time. If an investor waits to start saving, much more cash must be invested to achieve even a percentage of these results. The same is true for professional help in your marriage and parenting. The earlier you begin making the investment, the earlier the dividends begin and the more they can begin to build. The converse is also true; if you wait, you will spend much more money and emotional energy and gain only a portion of the results. Start where you are, and start today. The only difference between the financial chart and hiring a counselor is that you should never stop employing these professionals. We have been on this journey for thirty years and still employ the regular use of professional coaches and counselors of some sort.

If you have the right professional counselors and therapists on your team and listen to and act on their advice, three things will be true in your marriage and parenting journeys. First, you will have backup. There will be times when you know in your gut you are making the right calls but all of the voices around you and your children are crying foul; friends avoid you in the halls at church, and acquaintances offer a thousand suggestions. Don't worry; your professional team will back up your intuition.

Secondly, there will be times when you need a course adjustment. You will make a decision in anger or sadness. You will put all of your energy into a strategy you've read in a book or heard in a seminar, but it's not right for your marriage or your child. Your professional team will help you gain perspective. They will point you back to what you know to be true, and they will help you adjust

Resilience is about getting back up every time you go down.

fuzzy thinking into crystallized action. They will know you and remain far enough removed and unbiased to offer the perspective you need.

Thirdly, the right professional team will be your advocate. You'll have someone on your team when it's time to go nose-to-nose with your school over your child's Individualized Education Plan (IEP), when you need to convince an institution to work with you, when you have to go to court, when the police show up on your doorstep, or in a thousand other scenarios.

Your professional team of counselors and therapists will help you bounce back faster and stronger after life attempts to take you to your knees. Resilience is about getting back up every time you go down.

Standing Up: Resilience of Heart

The outcome of becoming more and more resilient is the ability to stand up on behalf of your spouse and your child. In counseling circles, they use the word *advocate* and call the process *advocating*. You will become your own best advocate. No expert, teacher, or professional knows your child like you do. *You are the expert on your child!* Don't let this scare you; all this means is that life is a contact sport, and it is not for children or adolescents. It takes adults. *You* are an adult. You are ready for the next period of play. You are *resilient*.

You will be your own best advocate. Note that I didn't say, "You will *have* to be." You are *already* the advocate for your child. Nobody has your mix of experiences, passion, love, and commitment. *Nobody.* You will be your own best advocate, no matter how many excellent professionals you have on your side. They won't be with you at all times, and they certainly won't be with you when you have to confront a child bodysurfing down your stairs at 2:00 a.m. You are your own best attorney, no matter how much bulldog your lawyer has in his or her bloodstream. You will have to know the laws, the regulations, and the medical procedures. You'll have to be your child's best teacher, because no matter how sharp the teachers are or how deep their understanding of learning styles and methods, you're the one best equipped to drive a lesson home. You will be there at the opportune and unexpected times when the teaching moments present themselves. You'll have to be your own best marriage therapist, because you know the depth of every issue and the history of every story in your marriage.

Standing up to life takes courage. You may think that courage only comes into play on the battlefield or at the scene of a car accident where you are thrust into a lifesaving role. Courage most often comes into play in the everyday events of life. It takes courage to say something difficult to your spouse or hold your tongue. It takes courage to set a fifth appointment with a teacher when you don't think you're getting through to her. It takes courage to keep telling a doctor about a medication that is not working.

Author and philosopher C. S. Lewis once wrote, "Courage is not simply one of the virtues, but the form of every virtue at the testing point, which means at the point of highest reality." Are you trying to always tell the truth? That's courageous. Are you trying to keep your family on an eating plan because you know the foods you've chosen are the right mix for your child? That takes courage. Are you trying to forgive your spouse even though they just made the same mistake for the thousandth time? You're living in a courageous marriage. You must have the courage to say no to a child and know that your spouse will support you. Courage and bravery come in many forms and can be developed more deeply. This is a lesson of one book on our suggested reading list, *Brave: 50 Everyday Acts of Courage to Thrive in Work, Love, and Life* by Margie Warrell.

Everyday resilience means knowing who you are and having enough self-confidence and courage to stand on your own two feet. Everyday resilience says, "I am willing to try, and if I fail today, I am willing to go out tomorrow and try again." Your life has to be characterized by getting knocked down and repeatedly getting back up. Always get up one more time than you fall. This is staying positive. This is resilience.

Pruning Thoughts: Resilience of Mind

I traveled to the Dominican Republic as a member of a dental team to perform treatment on those who had little access to dentistry. I was one of twenty dentists on the trip and much older than the twenty- and thirty-somethings in the group. We fell into a rhythm; we performed surgeries for eight to ten hours every day, and in the evening, we would review and discuss the day.

Each day started when we arrived at the makeshift clinic and greeted the growing line of patients. We would locate our workstations a few seconds before guides and translators would usher patient after patient to our chairs. Between surgeries, each dentist would stretch his or her back, drink water, and walk around the clinic floor.

Every day, I would walk past the chairs of my fellow dentists and wonder what procedures they were performing, and every day, I would pause beside a different chair because what I saw impressed me and challenged me as a dentist. Then, that night, I would quiz that dentist on the procedure. "How did you do that? What's the secret of making that work so smoothly? Why did that not cause more bleeding? Tell me about that instrument. How long does that take to heal? What continuing care is required?" Then, before bed, I would write notes in my journal recounting what I had learned and add my own thoughts.

One night, while discussing the excitement and challenge of an implant procedure, the dentist who had performed it sat down beside me. He said, "If I just listened to your voice and your questions, I would think you're in your thirties. You're inquisitive and act more like a dental student than you do a seasoned professional. You've got, what, almost forty years in practice?"

I hesitated, met his eyes, and replied, "There's always more I can learn. I can always do it better. I can be a better dentist. I can be a better businessman." I stopped and looked at the wobbling ceiling fan above us, then added, "I don't want anyone to ever say, 'Old Doc Thompson should've retired ten years ago.'"

I have a lot to learn about being a husband, a father, a brother, a son, an in-law, a friend, an employer, a dentist, a businessman, and a Christian. When I die, I can quit learning. For now, I will spend every day learning from Margrey, talking to wise people and life coaches, reading great books, going to counseling, taking notes from the sermons of our preacher, and being mindful of where I am in life. That's resilience of mind.

Resilience of mind also means unlearning and relearning certain lessons and at some point forgetting others. As parents and spouses, we have to unlearn or relearn as many ideas and concepts as we learned in the first place. We also have to put away just as many foolish ideas. Our growth sometimes looks like a tree getting seriously pruned. We have to prune ourselves, allow other professionals and peers to prune us, and invite our spouses to clip errant branches and leaves with the shears of honesty and compassion.

Even if you're not a sports fan, you've heard the phrase "rookie season," referring to the first year an athlete plays at the professional level. You've probably also heard of "veteran players" and "all-stars." In the journey to resilience as a spouse and as a parent of a special needs child, your rookie year may repeat often, every time you have to learn a new skill or your child reaches a new developmental level. That's the equivalent of playing multiple sports each season! Don't be too hard on yourself. Allow yourself to be a rookie in each new challenge you face. Over time, you will become a veteran player; you'll know when it happens, because you'll bear the bruises and sore muscles. Know that we will look upon you as an all-star and one of the heroes of parenting and marriage.

You and your spouse fully trust each other. You have committed to only success in all areas of marriage and parenting. You are focused on staying healthy in all dimensions of your life. You are choosing to be resilient. Like a rookie athlete, keep practicing, keep learning, and keep improving. Now it's time to laugh a little!

CHAPTER 7

CHOOSE OPTIMISM

A pessimist sees the difficulty in every opportunity;
an optimist sees the opportunity in every difficulty.
—*Winston Churchill*

ROY

You rise in the morning and have a choice every day: Will you focus on the good or dwell on the bad? Will you choose to be happy and encouraging to those around you, or will you be the downer in the room? Will you enjoy your career today or just view it as work that provides your necessary income? Will you laugh at life today?

Each of us has good *and* bad in our lives. We have triumphs and defeats; we have sunshine and rain. We can neither pick nor control the weather, but we can pick and control our *reaction* to the weather. We can learn to respond with more optimism and develop a better attitude as we mature if we choose to do so. We are creatures of choice, and we have a continuing habit of choosing our reactions to our circumstances. Selecting our reactions to what confronts us affects our lives and attitudes minute by minute and will change the direction and tone of our entire lives over time. When we allow negativity to rule our lives, we have lost control.

We cannot allow ourselves to be defined by our failures. Our failures are unwanted outcomes, but they do not define our lives. Our spouses and children deserve our most positive selves.

Studies show that when we allow life to control us, our stress and anxiety run rampant. Individuals who feel they have control over their lives are healthier, happier, and less likely to suffer from depression. When events don't go as planned, individuals who feel they have control look to what they did or didn't do that was responsible for the outcome. They take personal responsibility, and in doing so, they realize that in the future they can better control the outcomes of life events. On the other hand, many individuals tend to think that fate controls their lives or that external forces are what influence them. They feel they have no control, so they tend to question why they should try harder, when they have no power. Not only does this lead to a feeling of helplessness in life, but it also prevents people from giving themselves any credit when they have an unexpectedly great experience. They rob themselves of the positive emotions that come from celebrating victories in life.

As an example, a job interview may not end up successfully gaining someone employment. The individual who feels in control may inquire as to what the company was looking for other than the talent they brought to the table. They may look at how they performed in the interview or reassess their appearance and demeanor. Maybe they will look at whether they could have researched the company better or presented their credentials more positively.

Conversely, a person who feels fate controls their destiny may tend to think the company just wasn't hiring or that the person interviewing them may have been in a bad mood. Maybe they will think they were given bad information about the position or even that there were bad astrological alignments for an interview that day. The fate-oriented person will look for anything to explain away setbacks except something that they had control over. The person that faces life as controlled by fate feels that things just *happen* to them. Choose to feel you have control over your life, and you will more likely experience optimism.

In marriage, a couple becomes one, and they must act as one. This doesn't mean you become a clone of your spouse or lose your individuality; it *does* mean your philosophies should be compatible. Your mutual positivity as a couple will power you through rough days and unexpected events. You won't both be positive at all times, but as a rule, a habit and pattern of optimism will help you rise above the daily frays that come your way. When both spouses align themselves with positive attitudes and optimism, they are unstoppable! Within a mutually aligned couple, one of you can have an off day and still be supported by the other. When you both look for the good in situations, you can feed off each other's energy. Your synergy gives you more strength than when you are pulling against each other.

Choosing your attitude is a learned behavior. Where are you on the journey? Have you chosen optimism more than negativity? Do you respond with patience and grace when circumstances change, when bad news comes, and when things don't go your way? Where is your spouse on these spectrums? When outcomes are not to your liking, do you stop and see what can be learned from this life event, or do you pout and wallow in self-pity?

Choosing your attitude is simple, but not easy. Would you prefer to hang with friends that are positive and uplifting or with the Sad Sams and Sour Susies? When I'm not at my most ideal, optimistic self at the dental office, I ask myself, "Would I like to be my best friend today? Would I like to be an employee of me today?" Not once have I ever answered with even a tepid "yes." I shake my head and chuckle. Of course I don't want to be around myself when I'm in a less than stellar mood! So why would my friends, children, employees, and especially Margrey want to be around me on the days when I have a crappy attitude? Thus, I resolve to be more energetic and uplifting. I choose to be a lifter and pull others up, not be a leaner bearing down on them.

Furthermore, I give those around me permission to call me out (tenderly!) on my attitude. Sometimes we need a "check up from the neck up," as popular motivational author and speaker, Zig Ziglar was known to say. Patients are always asking me, "How are you, Doc?" My answer always includes a word like *wonderful, terrific, great, exceptional,* or *incredible,* but I close by saying I'm getting better. Never do I answer with "good" or "okay." I tell patients that when I'm only good, I don't need to be treating them; I need to go home and not be around anyone else, pulling them down. Am I fabulous every single day? Heck, no! Margrey and I subscribe to the fake-it-till-you-make-it attitude of the optimistic person. My employees and patients count on this daily from me as their leader and doctor. My spouse counts on this in her partner, and yours does also—and whether or not you realize it, your children count on you as well. Choose to be extraordinary today.

Cultivating an Optimistic Marriage

Most couples we've met are not the same when it comes to positive attitudes. Often, one spouse is more upbeat and optimistic than the other. This often becomes a source of irritation when difficulties arise. The optimistic spouse is viewed as taking a "Pollyanna" attitude or of not living in reality. The more negative spouse is considered to be dragging the situation down or hindering progress. Too often, we've seen these couples get bogged down in complaining (inside or out loud) about the other instead of banding together for the sake of the family. Couples working against each other are in a tug of war, while the issues facing them languish. Couples working together are pulling in the same direction against the issue, and they have greater success.

We've even met some couples where both spouses are negative most of the time, especially under stress. We feel sadness for them and for their children. These couples seem stuck in quicksand and struggle there without hope. Counselors have told us that our positive comments need to overshadow negative comments by a five-to-one margin—that is, we need to acknowledge someone five times more than we criticize them. Research on marriage by John Gottman shows that during a fifteen-minute videotaped conversation between husband and wife, there is a 94 percent chance of reliably predicting if they will stay married based on this 5:1 ratio.[7] In the work environment, employers recognize that the number-one reason for job dissatisfaction is a lack of appreciation from the employer. The 5:1 ratio holds just as true in the business world as it does in marriage. Following are three suggestions for fostering optimism as a couple.

Identify. Take a few minutes to discuss optimism with your spouse. Ask your spouse how they see you. Sometimes, our spouses see things in us or about us that we can't see ourselves. We might assume things that don't show on the outside. By asking them to evaluate you first, you will open the door in the conversation to discussing your spouse's optimism as well. After you've both figured out how optimistic or negative you are, take the next step. Discuss how you respond to situations together. What is your unified attitude when the waves crash? Are you more optimistic or more negative? If the answer happens to be negative, ask yourself, "What do I gain by my negativity?" Choose to change something small today to start your metamorphosis into a more positive person.

"When you quit learning, you may as well start building your pine box."

Consider. Think back on a recent conflict or difficulty you faced together. How did you approach it? How long did it take you to become optimistic or positive about the outcome? Did you actually get there? Consider how much you tugged against each other as opposed to working together. Take a few deep breaths, and then offer an opinion as to what you could've done differently and better. Hopefully your spouse will consider their struggles too and offer them up for conversation. When you are both presented with a problem and you have different reactions at different intensities, don't fault your spouse for having a different opinion or one stronger or weaker in intensity than yours. We all have different hot buttons. Discuss together what lesson can be learned from this event.

---

[7] Gottman, John, Why Marriages Succeed or Fail, 2012, Simon & Schuster.

Convert your differences into strength as a couple. There are always learning moments for you and your children. Margrey's father, W. G. Neal, always said, "When you quit learning, you may as well start building your pine box." Are you still learning something new daily?

Prepare. There's an old adage that says everyone is either coming out of a crisis, in the middle of a crisis, or in the quiet before a crisis. Another tough moment is ahead for you and your family. When—not if—it comes, what will you do differently? How will you stay on the positive side of the equation? How will you remain optimistic together? How will you put your backs against each other and fight off what attacks you?

Becoming an Optimistic Couple as Parents

Children are different. They are creatures of emotion. This is because of the differing timing of development of the part of the brain that controls logical decision-making (the cortex) and that which controls emotion (the limbic system). The limbic system is responsible for reward-seeking and is stimulated by social (i.e., peers) and emotional variables. The limbic system develops earlier and faster than the cortex, meaning that until the cortex can catch up with the limbic system, the desire for rewards and the demands of social pressures override rational thinking. The cortex doesn't catch up to the limbic system until age twenty-five.

Children have neither learned to tamp down the negative nor learned to be self-aware. We believe it is healthy to allow a child to experience the full range of emotions, both negative and positive. As parents, we have to teach them how to respond to these emotions. They must listen to their moods and learn from them or else be controlled by them throughout their lives. Emotions can hijack children and teens. We know many adults who were hijacked by their emotions as children, and they carry that struggle now as parents or grandparents. If that is part of your story, find someone to work with so you can move forward with self-confidence in your marriage and in your parenting role.

When a child is ruled by emotion, the good times are great and the bad times are—well, let us just say the bad times are *hard*. Pulling a child out of a funk is not an on-the-spot event; parents who model positivity and optimism throughout their own lives are able to help a child turn their attitude in a positive direction within minutes or hours, depending on the severity. A child quickly sees through a parent who is trying to "turn it on." The attempt at positivity can even backfire, and the parent and child slide deeper into the negative murk.

However, these suggestions are not meant to downplay a clinically depressed state; I'm not hinting that someone who is chronically depressed can simply wake up one morning and say, "I'll be happy from now on." Clinical and chronic depression are not the topic of this book; they are serious medical conditions that need to be addressed with psychological counseling and possibly pharmacological intervention. Clinical depression in either a child or a parent is serious and should be diagnosed and treated early.

Children often learn better from our examples than from our words. Lessons are more caught than taught. Therefore, it's impractical to tell a child to "cheer up" when you yourself are down. When our son Dylan was eight years old, we were having dinner and he stated that he didn't want to be a dentist. Being a dentist myself, I was curious, so I asked why. His statement had a profound impact on me from that point on in my life. He said, "Dad, you're always complaining about something at the office when you come home." That response was like a sucker punch in the gut to me. At that moment, I chose to change and emphasize the more enjoyable and positive things about my office in my evening conversations.

If you are telling yourself that you just aren't a motivating parent, or optimistic, or funny, then you can choose to change. Being motivational, positive, and optimistic is a choice you generally control. Margrey and I dated while I was in dental school; some of our dates were to social events with my classmates. Although Margrey knew only a few of my friends, she always talked to everyone and had more fun than I did. At some point I realized I was an introvert. Instead of accepting that I wouldn't be as outgoing as her, I chose to change. I began talking to people. I started asking them questions. I became more extroverted and had more fun. I'm still basically an introvert, but when called on, I can adapt to the situation at hand. I will never allow myself to accept the excuse that I'm just not a certain way. Don't allow yourself to make an excuse! Choose to change and become the parent your child needs and the partner your spouse wants, needs, and deserves.

Heather went through a "goth" stage in high school. She painted her fingernails black—not with polish but with a Sharpie. She wore black eyeliner and black lipstick and painted her binders and tennis shoes black. In case you are wondering, black is not the color of optimism! She wanted to wear only black clothes, and she tried, but Margrey refused to buy them in any significant amount. Heather scrawled class notes on her arms in all kinds of black ink. She would prefer to lock herself in her room and skip school. That's where one of our Thompson Family Values came into play: You go to school unless Margrey or I see vomit, blood, or a fever. The same rule applies to Margrey and me about work; feeling blue (or black) is not a ticket to stay home for a parent or child.

During Heather's dark stage, we knew our optimism and cheerfulness would need to be consistent and applied liberally across her life. Every morning, I would open the blinds wide in her room, letting the sunshine stream in, and I'd cheerfully greet her with my signature phrase, "Time to get up. It's going to be a great day!" Black eyes, nails, and attitudes continued, but our ongoing positivity finally wore Heather down. Don't roll your eyes! Of course, it's not as simple as we make it sound, but sometimes you've just got to laugh at the stuff these kids can come up with.

This less than ideal stage lasted longer than a year, and that year was tough on all of us. Behind our outward smiles and "good morning"s, we were stressed. When Margrey and I retired in the evening and reviewed our successes, we thought up new ways to battle Heather's attitude. We would flip coins to see who would have to go into her dungeon and wake her up. We would roll dice to see who would present the positive side of life on a particular day. We would draw straws to see who drove an hour with her in the car to an event, knowing she would not speak a word the entire time. We drove many trips in dead, dark silence. I even bribed Margrey at times to take a double shift of the silent treatment.

Throughout this stage, we were consistently worried about Heather's well-being. We didn't want to overlook signs of clinical depression. We were worried she might hurt herself. We stayed hypervigilant. Neither of us are psychologists, but together, we braved this storm—and all of us, especially Heather, came out unscathed.

Developing or Strengthening a Positive Attitude

Margrey and I can identify a pessimist within a few seconds. We've interviewed enough job candidates over the years to know a negative person at first glance. We've always had a rule: hire for attitude and teach skills. It has been our experience that the employee with the best attitude is much more teachable and easy to grow than one with better skills but unable to get along with others or in a mood that brings the team down. One bad apple really can spoil the whole basket.

If you would label yourself as a bit less than optimistic, there is hope; you can change, but it won't be an overnight transformation. It will help to partner with your spouse on this journey. Trust, commitment, and health will be your companions; optimism and resilience will go hand in hand.

Surround Yourself with Positive People. If you're of a more pessimistic bent, put yourself in the presence of optimistic people. You already know who they are; they probably drive you nuts at work, church, your child's ballgames, or PTA meetings. Quietly join their conversations and listen. How do they talk about and handle the situations that would wear you down? What words do they repeat? How do they carry themselves? Think about their facial expressions; without speaking, try to mirror their postures and smiles while standing there. Optimism can be contagious; unfortunately, so can negativity. Run with a positive crowd for a while, and watch as your own attitude improves. Tell yourself to smile. It takes many more facial muscles to frown than to smile! Take the easy route and smile. When someone inquires how you are doing, respond with "great" or "wonderful" or "exceptional." If you aren't doing great now, you will be soon. Zig Ziglar always said you aren't telling a story if you aren't doing so great; you're just telling the truth in advance. "I'm wonderful, but I'll improve throughout the day!"

Ask Better Questions—Be Mindful. Too often, we allow circumstances to rule our lives, our decisions, or our reactions. All we do is react—we don't think; we don't ask why; we don't seem to look for the learning opportunity in the situation. In the next couple of days, experiment with asking these questions about a few situations that come your way at work or home. See how they change your thinking. Many professionals refer to this as "being mindful" or "practicing mindfulness." Being mindful requires you to slow down and sense how you are reacting to your environment and why. If you are nervous or anxious, ask, "What has happened in the last hour to put me here?" If you are amped or jazzed up, ask, "Why?" If you are happy or optimistic, ask yourself, "What is causing this feeling?" Mindfulness requires slowing down your mind and thinking with introspection.

Consider the following questions to see how you can be more present in the moment:

- What are two or three positive outcomes that could naturally result from this issue?
- What strengths do I bring to this situation?
- Who do I know that could help?
- When something like this happened before, what came to pass?
- What good could come from this?
- Should I let this situation unfold on its own?

Find Spirituality. There is personal empowerment in recognizing that a power greater than yourself guides this world and is in control. As discussed in a previous chapter, find a support group that embraces your spiritual belief system, and become an active part of it. Make certain that this is a positive and uplifting group. Whether you call it meditation, prayer, mindfulness, or self-awareness, spend some quiet time reflecting on the positives in your life. Express gratitude daily for your blessings. Everyone has something to be grateful for in life.

Read or Listen to Self-Improvement and Motivational Books. There are too many books in the world to read in one lifetime. Whatever issue brings you down, you can find dozens of motivational books to lift you up. Your book selection need not be a five-hundred-page epic. You can be inspired by many books with simple vocabularies and fewer than one hundred pages. If you are not a reader, then change! Surveys show that nearly 30 percent of Americans read one book or less each year. Turn off the TV and become a reader and lifelong learner.

If you don't care to read, listen to audiobooks. If you have a commute, long or short, audiobooks can be a great benefit. In a fifteen-minute drive to the office, you get two-and-a-half hours of listening time each week. Many audiobooks can be listened to at up to twice the normal reading pace. In a year, you can easily listen to twenty or more audiobooks.

Tell Yourself a Better Story. When something upsets or derails us—maybe a confrontation with a co-worker or a spat with a spouse—our brains scramble to turn it into a story. Giving an incident a beginning, middle and end is a pattern the brain recognizes and rewards.

But here's the thing: A lot of the stories we tell ourselves just aren't true, says Brené Brown, a Houston social worker and best-selling author.

"Let's say I have a bad meeting at work with Maggie," offers Brown. "In a split second my brain says, 'I knew that Maggie didn't like me.' And then we take off from there. When we're in struggle and uncertainty, our emotions are driving while our thoughts and behavior are in the back seat. If we can't catch that story and reality-check it, it will take us places we don't want to go."

Brown, a fifth-generation Texan, has built her career on places people don't want to go. Years of research on shame and vulnerability—interviewing men and women about their darkest demons, sometimes as tears stream down their cheeks—have led to books that pack exhaustive research with personal stories, pop-culture touchstones and Texas-style straight talk.

Brown's best-selling "Daring Greatly" (2012) focused on vulnerability and the difficult but rewarding process of stepping into the arena and letting yourself be seen. That book helped birth her new title, "Rising Strong," a guide to getting back up after trying and failing.

Brown divides her "Rising Strong" process into three parts that look tidy on paper but, in practice, may take days, months or years of slogging through personal sludge to change your life:

The reckoning: Get curious about how your emotions connect with the way you think and behave.

The rumble: Get honest about the stories you're making up about your struggles and challenge yourself to determine what's truth, what's self-protection and what must change to live a "wholehearted" life.

The revolution: Write a new ending to your story based on what you learned in the rumble and improve the way you engage with the world.[8] Rewrite a better story for yourself.

Recently, Molly traveled with a group on an adventure trip. I was sitting at home checking my email when one popped up from the chaperone, with the subject line, "Molly is okay, but . . ." I actually called Margrey into the study and asked if I should open the email or delete it. In the five seconds it took to begin reading, only negative thoughts entered my mind. The event actually was insignificant and the email almost unnecessary. Molly and her friends had gotten into an argument initiated by some attention seeking behavior that had disrupted their relationships. It was humbling to recognize how fast we wrote a negative story before gathering the facts. Even Margrey and I struggle to write the most optimistic story at times, and we must remind ourselves that we focus on progress, not perfection.

At one point, Molly was physically assaulted by another child. Molly's psychologist, who specialized in cognitive training, worked to empower

---

[8] Brown, Brené, Rising Strong, 2015, Spiegel & Grau, A book review by Maggie Galehouse.

her to rewrite the narrative around the assault. Over several months of therapy, a new story was written from a factual position, reflecting the good decisions that she made during the incident. The therapy focused on allowing Molly to see the excellent decisions she made during the assault, which showed personal empowerment even during a bad situation. In conjunction with the police, the court system, and her school, Molly regained strength and persevered. She was shown how to avoid being defined by a single experience and how to move past it.

As a parent and as an individual, you can rewrite your story. In Jim Loehr's *The Power of Story*, the author details how you can write your narrative to be more empowered and create the life you desire and deserve. Define your core values and your personal mission—or redefine them—to become the parent and spouse your family deserves. Loehr masterfully guides you through the process necessary to change your story and, as a result, transform your life to what you want it to be instead of what it is at present. Mr. Loehr goes far beyond telling you to change and

Staying optimistic is a lifelong choice and requires continual work. Positivity makes a difference, and perseverance is the key.

shows how, through recreating your story, your destiny in life can be altered.[9] His book is powerful for anyone interested in self-improvement.

Persevere. If you've been a negative force for a long time, your children won't buy the new, optimistic you at first. It will take time. Persevere! Don't let their negative reactions and comments about your newfound positive view cause you to retreat to your old grumpy style. Over time, they will accept the change and move forward with you. Once you're optimistic with your spouse, you must keep talking and solving problems. Keep a unified and positive front. Put your backs together and fight off what confronts you. Staying optimistic is a lifelong choice and requires continual work.

---

[9] Loehr, Jim, The Power of Story, 2007, Free Press.

In our family, standard nightly dinners involved us gathering at the kitchen table with the TV and cell phones off. Each night we would ask open-ended questions during the meal—which, occasionally, were minimal due to our exhaustion. I know we just told you to eat nutritiously, but when the world has beat you too far down, it is okay to serve cereal for dinner occasionally. During Heather's quiet years, she would sometimes answer one of our questions with just a word or two; we would pounce on the answer and say, "Tell us more." If we got another sentence, we'd follow up with, "Really? What else?" If her answers were short or negative, we responded with an exuberant (although occasionally sarcastic), "Thank you for sharing that."

In addition to meals, we planned short family trips that required a drive of thirty minutes to an hour to get us out of the house. Conversations seemed to happen more naturally in the car and somehow engaged the children. We went bike riding with the younger kids, which isn't an expensive activity. The blood started pumping, the breeze felt good, and attitudes could change for a mile or two.

Activities like these would keep negativity at arm's length for a time. We looked forward to every night, when the daily grind was over and the kids were in bed. We would retire to the peace of our bedroom and consider the next day. We chose to express our inability to motivate or our frustration behind closed doors. We admitted our vulnerability to each other, but the children saw only upbeat parents. Positivity makes a difference, and perseverance is the key.

MARGREY

Learn to Laugh (At Yourself, Especially). Humor and laughter will keep you sane. Children need to laugh too, so lighten up! You must have a lot of optimism—not simply a day, a week, or a month. Laughter decreases stress hormones and increases immune cells and infection-fighting antibodies, thus improving your resistance to disease. Laughter triggers the release of endorphins, the body's natural feel-good chemicals. Endorphins promote an overall sense of well-being and can even temporarily relieve pain. The benefits of laughter are well documented in research. With children, there is always something to laugh about. With teens, there is even more to laugh about! If you don't laugh, you may cry.

Teaching Molly better language skills was an ongoing project in our family. We had basic knock-knock joke books in every car. While Roy was driving, I would read a joke out loud; Roy would explain the joke to Molly; and I would deliver the punchline. Molly would finally laugh, while the older children would roll their eyes. Regardless, we caught them laughing at these stupid jokes occasionally, and then we would *all* be laughing, including Molly. To this day, Molly still enjoys some of these jokes.

Life isn't just about laughing your way to optimism. Roy and I did— and still do—argue at times. We argued in front of the children. Most often, when we were legitimately discussing something, our passion for our views came across to the children as an argument. As young children, they would tell us to quit arguing. We were surprised, and we would tone down our passion. There were times during our family counseling appointments where the children would say, "Mom and Dad argue." The therapist would always bring the children back to the realization that we may have argued, but we always resolved our disagreements amicably and still respected and loved each other. Sometimes we didn't like each other after an argument, but we always loved and respected each other and insisted on each other's right to an opinion. It is important that children see their parents resolving conflict so that they don't grow up with the unrealistic expectation that marriage doesn't involve disagreement at times. This is the reality of marriage. Often, our arguments ended in laughter of some type. In retrospect, we argued about the most ridiculous things!

ROY

As a father I will forever remember one Sunday morning when Heather came into the kitchen dressed for church. She wore a hot pink minidress and black lace stockings. I blinked my eyes and gathered my breath, because she didn't look remotely like the Heather I knew. She looked a bit . . . *cheap*. Margrey simply stated that her attire was unacceptable, while I physically blocked the back door (Heather's exit from the house). Not only was she not going to church like that, she wasn't leaving the house like that—ever! Church was required—another Thompson Family Value—so she relented and changed clothes. I accepted her second choice of dress, whatever it was, just so Margrey and I could have the appearance of a win that morning. Out of her sight, we laughed. We thank God that we never saw that outfit again!

Years ago, we realized that life is too short to get bogged down in negativity. We learned to take what we do seriously (marriage, careers with patient care, raising children) but rarely to take *ourselves* too seriously. We make mistakes and laugh at them. We laugh at what we've been through with the children or within our marriage.

No matter what you're facing, there will be an end to the struggle. This is a reminder to be optimistic. No matter what you face—good or bad or terrible or even Goth—it will pass. Never forget that you and your spouse are a winning team. You can slay dragons together! With your spouse watching your back, you can fight the world and win. Difficult children can wear down a strong couple and win a battle or two, but together, parents always win the war. That win consists of emotionally stable, resilient, optimistic, and healthy parents that can't be separated. Never ever let a child get between the two of you. Choose laughter and optimism daily.

CHAPTER 8

NO EXCUSES

He that is good for making excuses is seldom good for anything else.
—Benjamin Franklin

ROY

One Saturday morning I got up and didn't run. I told myself that with rain in the forecast, it would be too messy. My friends had decided not to run either, so if I chose to go, I'd be going solo. I promised myself I'd have a good rainy day to get on the stationary bike—or take the day to swim or lift weights. I worked through the morning at my desk, cleaning clutter and writing part of this book. At noon, I ate lunch, and I really didn't want to exercise right away, so I read for an hour. At 2:30 p.m., I ran errands. At 8:30 p.m., I still hadn't exercised. Who do I have to blame? The weather, my lazy friends, too many errands that Margrey could have run instead of me? Any of these could get my finger pointing. Several times that day, I chose not to get dressed and exercise. I made a choice, albeit a small one, to not bother with my workout. It was my choice alone.

Margrey and I believe that most of what happens in our lives results from a combination of choices we make daily. They may be small decisions or complete changes in the direction of our lives, but they all come from some decision we've made—or, often, our failure to make a decision (which in its own way is a decision). Margrey and I feel that we can choose to trust and we can choose commitment, health, resilience, and optimism. If we aren't fully engaged just yet, we can choose to work on these factors or we can delay our progress and put off our improvement.

Choice is a matter of self-discipline. If you can't make these five choices, then you need to take this book to a counselor and say, "Help us get these five things figured out." Your journey may be like a ball of string that you must unravel to the beginning of to make sense of your life. It may take many years for you to loosen the ball, but do it! Don't hesitate; don't procrastinate. Meet with a trusted psychiatrist or psychologist and unravel that ball of string! You have less potential to succeed in marriage and parenting in a healthy fashion if you have unresolved issues of your own. One of our children's psychiatrists once told us that they typically spend the first year of therapy working on one or both parents, getting *them* healthy, before they can start helping the child.

I can make excuses just as well as the next person. I can "try" to do something. On more than one occasion, I've answered one of the children's requests with, "Yes, I can *try* to do that." The children, even when they were young, responded by saying, "That means you're probably not going to do it." That really hurt, but sometimes the truth hurts! "Try," to me, is as good as "no." How would you feel if your employer told you he or she was going to "try" to pay you on Friday? Would you be confident that a paycheck was coming your way? We are often reluctant to say we will do something and couch our responses with, "I don't know what the future holds, so I can't promise." When we say "try," that is our way out of a commitment. Choosing commitment isn't just about staying married. Choosing commitment is about reputation and character.

I was at a local business recently and wished the clerk a great day. She said it probably wouldn't be a great day because she might be losing her job. When I asked why, she told me she was late to work two or three times a week. She said she liked her job, but when I gently inquired why she was late, she said she just couldn't seem to get up on time.

I suggested she set her alarm fifteen minutes earlier so she could be timely, impress her employer, and keep her job. She looked at me like I had just landed from Mars. She said she just wasn't a morning person, so getting up earlier was not an option. I walked away thinking about how many other excuses I could have heard. The right choice is not always easy, but it always puts you on the right track. Tell yourself often: progress, not perfection.

I'm confident that with the right communication, you and your spouse can build more trust and come to commit fully to the long-term success of your marriage. This will take time if there is currently little trust between you; yet you can extend trust and commitment in order to start the process. Even without your spouse's involvement, you can choose a healthier lifestyle that will lead to more engaged and energized days. Your children, your employer, your coworkers, and your friends will appreciate your 100-percent renewed enthusiasm for life. You will develop resilience, and when you choose optimism and laughter, your life will be enriched. You will become someone others look up to and admire. In the face of adversity in raising difficult children, others will see you as their mentor. Your marriage will deepen, and you will become a better parent.

These are generally small choices made daily, but when you start down this path, your life changes. As with the process of losing weight, you may not see a daily change, but when you look back over time, you will see and experience a new you. The old Chinese proverb from philosopher Lao Tzu says that "the journey of a thousand miles begins with a single step.[10]" Grab the hand of your spouse, and together, choose to take that first step today.

The motion picture industry rocked along in black and white for years. Silent films gave way to talkies; then color showed up. The first color movies were filmstrips bathed in washes of color before being projected; then artists started painting each individual frame. The dull and

---

[10] Tzu, Lao, Tao Te Ching.

pale colors thrilled audiences, but full color didn't arrive until Technicolor. Technicolor's first enduring achievement was *The Wizard of Oz*. Early in the story, a twister sweeps Dorothy and her farmhouse from Kansas all the way to the land of Oz. When she woke up and emerged from the house and the screen shifted from the browns and grays of the Kansas dustbowl to a prism full of color in Oz, audiences gasped.

We pray for many Technicolor moments in your family. You have a good black-and-white picture of what you need to think and believe; sure, there are many gray areas, but the major ideas are outlined. Now it's time to bring those to light in the day-to-day world of your family. The philosophies and beliefs outlined previously have to be in place, or else all the creative ideas in the world won't be effective.

It's not enough to believe the right things or even be able to articulate them in conversation. You must put them into action. You must *show up*. You must act. Imagine if someone read many books on money management and memorized many rules and quotes about it but never put any of it into action. As medical practitioners, we've experienced this over and over again with our patients. Action is required for real change to occur.

As a dentist, I am often asked by patients if I'm doing a procedure for the first time. A patient wants reassurance that this isn't my first rodeo. Early in my career, this was a tough question, because at some point there is a first time for *any* procedure. Through the years I have come to answer the question and think about it differently. Now my answer is always, "Yes, this is the first time for this procedure." In dentistry, any tooth, on any patient, on any day, with any amount of decay, always presents a first time, so I explain to patients that I've done hundreds of procedures similar to theirs but never one on an identical tooth. My plan with all patients is to provide a painless and successful outcome on their procedure. I've never had a patient refuse treatment when I've explained in this way.

By now, you may be a bit curious about what happened in each of our children's escapades we shared earlier.

Heather and the Principal

When Margrey and I got to the principal's office to see what Heather had done, we discovered that none of my initial speculations were close to the truth. This occurred early in the years of the internet, pre-Facebook. The school had sponsored a speaker who presented a message to the student body. Heather had written a blog on the internet about it, found and uploaded a photo of the speaker from a website, and mentioned several students by name in her post. Margrey and I read the post over the principal's shoulder. I kept expecting to read something sensational, malicious, or derogatory about the speaker or the students mentioned. Nothing! There had to be another shoe about to drop. I remained quiet, because the principal had all the power in this meeting. I am a rule follower. My job in this forum was to support the authority figure in the situation.

"Dr. and Mrs. Thompson," the principal stated, "we feel that the privacy of the students mentioned in the post has been violated. Furthermore, Heather has stolen a picture of the speaker from a website, which breaks our school's honor code and places liability for its use on the school."

Margrey and I looked at each other. I got the feeling that both of us were relieved at the news, but inside I was seething. The principal continued, "Heather needs to open her computer so I can watch her delete the post, the photographs, and any other internet material pertaining to this incident."

I sat there, quiet yet consumed by self-doubt. I was also thinking about the dozens of journals at home that Heather had spent hours writing in. She cherished what she wrote. There was nothing inflammatory about this writing; indeed, I wondered how many people had even seen the post. I wanted to cross the principal. I also wondered, *Does Margrey expect more leadership from me right now?*

I watched as Heather did what the principal demanded. The text and images disappeared before our eyes. The principal was satisfied, Heather didn't seem too beat up by the incident, and Margrey and I headed to the car to go home.

I couldn't hold back anymore. "Are you kidding me?" I ranted. "I canceled patients for this. Does the principal not realize we are in a new digital world? This is the type of petty nonsense that you and I just shrug off. How can the principal get into these weeds? We need our energies for the wars to come, not the equivalent of a firecracker."

I kept going for another fifteen miles before Margrey began to laugh—and then I laughed. We laughed together, and the moment passed. We needed Heather in this school for her success, and Heather agreed that she would learn from the incident. The more we thought about it, the more we realized that the name of the school and the identity of students openly mentioned on the internet *should* be of grave concern to the school. Plus, we could appreciate that they would protect our child the same way they were protecting these other students. Besides, neither sex nor drugs was involved; nothing was stolen, broken, vandalized, or burned down. Heather was safe. I wasn't even sure it was a violation of the honor code, but at this point I didn't care. Looking back, I realize Heather was on the cutting edge of blogging.

As parents of special needs children, we must choose our battles wisely. Not every hill is worth dying on. For a while, I wanted to draw my sword in this battle, but I kept it in the scabbard. Margrey held back too. Together, we lived to fight a more intense battle on another day.

MARGREY

Dylan and His Classmate

As Dylan and I walked down the hall, he told me what he had said to the other boy: "I wish we had never abolished slavery." You guessed it; Dylan said it to an African American classmate (who happened to be twice his size), and the two of us were headed down the hall to meet with a polished and efficient principal (who happened to be African American herself). I gripped his arm and said, "You know better! You've been taught better!"

I wanted to say much more but the Holy Spirit—and my teeth—held my tongue.

The principal sat Dylan down and said, "There's only one name you should call another person at this school, and it's the name their parents gave them." Apparently Dylan had made some very inappropriate comment to his classmate.

I nodded my agreement and waited for her to say more. Then I was surprised.

"Mrs. Thompson," she said, "You'll have to leave the room now. I want to talk directly to these boys. This is now a matter between them and me."

I was happy to leave the principal's office. That was fine by me. I never found what conversation the principal had with Dylan but the incident ended there in her office.

This story exposed Dylan's early-life biases toward women and minorities. We had recognized Dylan's biases in the first few months after his adoption, when he was just four years old. Roy and I now realized that sexist or biased comments in any form could be easily mimicked or exaggerated by Dylan. His early years biased him toward a behavior and attitude that is not tolerated in our family. Even though Dylan was in third grade, we realized we had work to do in shaping his future behavior and attitudes towards others. Through the years with constant attention to embracing diversity, Dylan has grown into a respectful adult.

ROY

Molly and the Car

Remember my neighbor Claudia calling about Molly driving Margrey's car around the neighborhood? My first question on the phone that day was, "Claudia, can you get the keys from Molly?"

"I've raised three boys. I'm certain I can get the keys," Claudia said.

I arrived home at my regular time, around 5:30 p.m. Molly looked sheepishly up at me and said, "You've talked to Ms. Claudia already, haven't you?"

My powerful parenting question followed. "Why would you say that?"

"I made a bad decision today. I got Mom's car and went for a drive."

"Are you ever going to do that again?"

"No, sir."

That was good enough. She simmered in the shame of it for about two more hours. She had sweated all afternoon, and I could tell she was remorseful. Margrey had warned me a week before to exercise more caution with the car keys. "Molly is really looking at those car keys a lot," she had told me. Lesson learned by Roy: I should listen more intently to my wife! Molly never took the car again; I never left the keys out again. It took me several days to get over my own embarrassment to get the keys back from Claudia.

When you parent and participate in marriage, you will rarely encounter exactly the same problem twice. Don't assume from this statement that your children will learn each lesson the first time. That will rarely happen. Rather, each time an opportunity arises to teach a child or learn something about your marriage, the situation will be slightly different. This is where your skill as a parent can flourish. You must be quick and agile and pull from all your previous experiences to succeed. You will not always perform at 100 percent, but each encounter will make you faster, better, and stronger. Always be on the road to improvement; never accept or make excuses.

CHAPTER 9

PREGAME EVERYTHING

Give me six hours to chop down a tree and I will spend the first four
sharpening the axe.
—*Abraham Lincoln*

ROY

I arrived at home one Thursday around 6:00 p.m. to find Margrey screaming at the kids, who at the time were ages four to ten. I was surprised. In
our earlier parenting years, we may have lost our temper or raised our
voices, but by this time we had matured and typically were more reserved
and contemplative. I put my stuff down and quickly but tenderly suggested that she allow me to take care of the children for the rest of the
evening. I could see she was at her wit's end. She needed a break from the
children, and the children needed a break from her. I couldn't imagine
what had gone so wrong since 3:00, when the kids had been picked up
from school. I helped them with the rest of their homework, wrote notes
to teachers, and helped get backpacks loaded and put by the back door.
After baths and teeth-brushing, I read stories and then put them to bed
around 9:00 p.m. I must admit I was feeling pretty impressed with my
husbanding and parenting skills!

Fast-forward two days to Saturday: Margrey left to run an errand at 10:00 a.m. I had the kids corralled, and we were having a fun time that morning—no homework, no to-do list, and everyone still in their pajamas. I got to spend time preparing my famous homemade animal-shaped buckwheat pancakes. Two hours later, Margrey returned—and the house was in chaos. I had each child in time-out; I may have resorted to spanking; dishes were on every kitchen counter; leftover pancakes and syrup decorated the table; and *I'm screaming.* Margrey gently smiled and suggested I separate myself from the children, and inside, I knew for a fact that she was laughing at me. Two days previously, she'd had the children after a full day of school and three hours of homework and lost her patience. My patience was extinguished on an easy Saturday morning within two hours! I realized I still needed to work on that humility stuff, and maybe I needed to learn more in the areas of patience and parenting too.

What went wrong in this scenario was *the pregame plan.* Everything in a family with difficult children needs pregaming. Pregaming helps in every family, in your career, and in everything in your life. Even Saturday mornings need some amount of pregaming! We learned that it was a must to discuss—with the children, in advance—our lives, upcoming events, and activities. Our children do not transition easily; when they are tired, they don't transition at all. Most adults can switch from activity to activity with ease. Children, and even teens, do not do this as easily. As adults, we have developed a sense of self-awareness. When we are struggling, we instinctively know better than children and teens how to back off and take a breath. When you are tired *and* the children are tired, a pregame plan still gives you some hope of success.

I'm not a sports aficionado, but I've turned on the TV enough to see the NFL pregame show at 11:30 on Sunday mornings. The hosts are discussing all the day's games; they are breaking down what the running backs, the quarterbacks, and both teams' defensive and offensive linemen will have to do to prevail. They discuss what the opposition backfield will have to do to stop the opposing team. They discuss weaknesses and how each team will have to work to succeed against its opponent. They are analyzing an intricate puzzle to give us their best expectation of the outcome of the game. Pregaming in sports results in a win for one team and a loss for the other. In your family, pregaming brings success for everyone when carried out well.

In the week leading up to a game, the team is studying tapes of its opposition. They are repeatedly running drills and practicing special plays. The basics can never be abandoned, but practice in all areas—physical, mental, and emotional—helps their chances of winning the game. The same applies to your family dynamic. Never forget the pregame plan.

In dentistry, as in any profession, a skilled operator can complete a procedure nearly automatically when everything goes well or is routine. As a surgeon, your skill shows when something goes wrong or when complex procedures are necessary. Systems in the office help make everything appear to run smoothly on the outside. One of the greatest compliments our patients give my team is when they say we all work seamlessly together and seem to flow through an appointment.

A system helps, but a pregame plan for a difficult procedure prepares everyone on the team. When we have a procedure scheduled in the office that is complex, I will type out a detailed timetable of expectations in advance. This is reviewed with my assistants prior to the appointment. This timetable may remind the whole staff about a special instrument we'll need for the procedure or if there's any part of it that may present an unusual situation. This timetable also includes when each part of the procedure will occur. Routinely, these procedures result in a successful clinical outcome. A pregame plan with your family will be equally successful.

When the children were young, sometimes they came to business functions or meetings with us. If we were out in public, we would often run into people we knew—friends, business acquaintances, or patients. We told the children beforehand that we would introduce them. They were taught to shake hands with people, look them in the eye, and greet them in whichever way was most comfortable. We prepped the children to call people "Mr." or "Mrs.," regardless of what the individual said to call them. We suggested that people they meet might ask them some questions: "How old are you?" "What grade are you in?" "Where do you go to school?" "Who's your teacher?" "What's your favorite subject?" On multiple occasions, after meeting people in public, our kids would express amazement that we could predict what people were going to ask them. Our goal was to set the children up for success, not failure. Pregaming is just as simple, but it has to be remembered and carried out routinely.

If we went to the movies, Margrey and I would refuse to engage in any type of arguments while there, especially about concessions. To prevent them, we would stop at the convenience store. and each child got to choose a sweet to bring to the movie. We told the children they could all share a drink, but there would be no popcorn. We never had a scene at the theater. At times, we even discussed the seating arrangement before we went into the theater. Everyone went to the bathroom prior to watching the movie. We rarely had to leave the theater due to a child's meltdown. That's not always been the case when we went out.

My sister Cheryl and her husband, Robbie, have five intelligent and well-behaved children. When their kids were growing up, Robbie always kept five playing cards in the van. Anytime they were headed out together, the children got to draw cards. The child that drew the highest card got to pick where they wanted to sit, and the process continued until the child that got the lowest card took the remaining seat. This is such a simple pregame, and it was used on children who did not have special needs! All children and their parents can benefit from the pregame plan.

One Saturday morning, I took all three children to IHOP for pancakes. Once we arrived, the wait was moderate, but the service was a bit slow. The children couldn't decide what to order—chocolate-covered pancakes with whipped cream and cherries, chocolate milk or orange juice, or eggs and bacon that I knew wouldn't be eaten. We all grew frustrated, and they were acting like spoiled kids. We ate and left. I tipped heavily as penance for the distraction to other diners. In the car, I expressed my disappointment that they didn't appreciate me taking them out to eat. Inside my heart, I cried, and I was embarrassed that I had done absolutely no pregaming, thus ensuring a failed experience. I apologized to the children, and we discussed how next time could be more enjoyable. The learning, when we parent, should be bigger than the experience.

Sometimes the children had to be dropped off at one of our offices for a few hours. We prepared them by letting them know that they would be in our private office and should stay there. We gave them books, games, and snacks and reinforced the questions that everyone would ask. Generally, it worked, but when Dylan was ten years old, he was found playing with a drill in the dental lab at my office. My assistant suggested he not play with the drill, but Dylan ignored her. She then told him outright to stop playing with the drill. Dylan looked at her and said, "My dad is your boss, and you are a worker." She was confident in our relationship, and the next day she told me about it. Dylan spent the following Saturday on his hands and knees, cleaning the laboratory floor. I reminded him that when one of my team members gave him a direction, it was as good as if it had come from Mom or me.

I had failed Dylan by not setting the rules and pregaming, yet he had been grossly insubordinate to an adult something he should have known better than to do. Sometimes you will fail to pregame everything, and full-on insubordination may happen. Because of the incident with the drill, I learned that I needed to make sure that the children always knew directions from the nanny, babysitter, or any team members of mine or Margrey's were as good as our word.

Pregaming church was routine. Who would sit where? Could the older children sit with friends or invite their friends to sit with us? We let them know that wherever they sat, we would have eyes on them. We visited the bathroom prior to church and Sunday school so that no one had the need (or the excuse) to leave in the middle of a service or class. They were given money to put in the collection plate, and through pregaming, they knew to have it ready. They knew to stand up to sing and not to talk during a prayer.

One Sunday at church, when Heather was fourteen years old, she sat four rows in front of us with a friend. During the service, they kept whispering to each other and were oblivious to the sermon. As the ushers went forward for the contribution, I snuck into the aisle toward them and stopped behind where Heather was sitting. I leaned in and tapped the two girls on the shoulder and said, "If the two of you snicker once more or talk during a prayer, I'll come back and escort you both out of the auditorium. That will be very embarrassing for both of you. Do you understand me?"

"Yes, sir," Heather promptly replied. Her friend didn't respond, so I addressed her: "Do you understand me also?"

"Yes, sir." I returned to my seat, and the service was quite enjoyable thereafter. Several friends that morning acknowledged that I had the courage to discipline my child and someone else's child quietly but firmly in the middle of church. If we had pregamed the situation better, we might have avoided this incident.

Don't get me wrong, though; pregaming doesn't always ensure success. On more occasions than not, Molly was disruptive in church despite our best pregaming efforts. Friends behind us would jokingly tell us they could tell what kind of mood she was in by how much room we gave her on the church pew. On more than one occasion, I carried Molly, screaming, out of the auditorium. Thank goodness she never screamed, "Please, Dad, don't beat me. I promise I'll behave." It always can be worse than what you imagine!

Planning a road trip without a pregame plan is the equivalent of driving headlong into a tornado. When we traveled, we always pregamed heavily. Travel is stressful for everyone and can wear the most seasoned road warrior down. Margrey would pack the kids' backpacks with snacks, coloring books, markers, playing cards, puzzles—any trinket that would occupy them even for a few minutes would go into their backpacks. They were never allowed to peek into their backpacks until we were at the airport gate or well on the road in the car. We wrote car rules, and when the children were old enough to read, we taped them on the back of the seat in front of each of them. We had trash bags rigged in the van in multiple places.

Once, on a multiday driving vacation, we had carnival tickets, and we gave the kids a list of what they could do to earn a ticket. They were told they could exchange each ticket for a quarter, and the money could be used for their souvenirs. This was money we were already planning to provide for souvenirs, but we incorporated the money into this behavior plan.

On a subsequent eight-hour drive to Florida, we gave nickels to the children anytime they used the proper tone of voice or said something nicely or complimented a sibling in the car. That money could be used to "buy" food that we had packed in a cooler for the trip. We "sold" Hershey's Kisses, gum, candy bars, soda, and sandwiches for twenty-five cents each. We made sure they never earned enough to overindulge but could buy enough snacks so we didn't have to stop for food on the way. I'll always remember Heather saying something like, "Dylan, can you please pass the DVD?" and Dylan responding, "I'd be glad to, Heather." They both would then wait for a nickel. Not to be outdone, their younger sibling Molly would chime in, "Y'all are both so nice! Do I get a nickel also?"

> *Pregaming doesn't guarantee success, but it gives your family a fair chance on most occasions.*

Maybe this sounds simplistic, but in reality, it can be straightforward. However, when you are one hundred miles down the road and everyone is screaming and fighting (and we have seen that also), it is hard to turn that scenario into a calm drive. Pregaming doesn't guarantee success, but it gives your family a fair chance on most occasions.

Here are some situations where pregaming might come in handy:

- Ride to school
- Field trips/school activities
- Vacations
- Community events
- Playground or biking activities
- Sporting events
- Homework/study time
- Chores around the house/cleaning their rooms
- Visits to medical professionals

- Standardized tests at school
- Family visits
- Holidays
- Errands

Do you feel pregaming with your spouse would help in certain instances? What about meetings with teachers at school? You will see in a later chapter more suggestions for school meetings, but here are some ideas to consider. First, who will go with you? Who will carry the conversation? Who will be the good guy and who the bad guy? Will you leave the talking to the attorney? What questions will you ask, and where will you compromise on your child's Individualized Education Plan?

Do you pregame prior to looking at a new car or heading to a family reunion? We still pregame Christmas. In September or October, we discuss together our budget and what the children need or want. We negotiate what gifts will be given now or what may be better saved for later in the next year (such as for a birthday). Margrey and I pregame social events, especially an event at our house. Weeks ahead, we have discussed what food will be served and who will prepare it. Closer to the event, we discuss more details: When will the food be served? What drinks should be offered? Who will serve? Where will we seat our guests? Are candles lit? Who answers the door? And if the children are at home, what are they allowed to do while our guests are there (yes, they always had a babysitter upstairs with them!)? Imagine having friends over for dinner and, upon their arrival, asking your spouse, "What are we serving tonight? Why don't you run to the store and grab some stuff?" Sound crazy? I'm sure you have seen something similar happen.

Here are some more pregame suggestions:

1. Plan, plan, and plan ahead. This cannot be overemphasized. If one or both parents are rushing at the last minute, you could be doomed.
2. Review what went wrong on a prior occasion. Without pointing fingers, brainstorm what could have been done differently.

3. Review a time everything went smoothly, and make notes of why it went well.

4. Choose one or two things to fix at a time.

5. Observe what motivates your children and plan rewards or consequenses accordingly.

6. Ask your psychiatrist or psychologist for his or her perspective and ideas for betterment.

7. Think about your children's transitions. Slow their lives down just a little. Allow extra time to get everyone out the door.

8. Discuss with your physician altering medication doses for late-night events, long trips, airline flights, special family events, or vacation schedules.

9. Create a mental picture of the outcome you envision. Expect success, but be prepared for failure.

10. Before an event, be ready well in advance.

11. Physically separate your children for successful outcomes. We had separate teeth-brushing stations in the morning to eliminate fights before school.

12. Discuss with the kids what the following day or week will look like. Get them involved in the pregame warm-up. (Note that there were times we didn't share anything in advance so they wouldn't be distracted from the present day's events. Use your judgment.)

13. Be ready to bail out. There may be times when you'll need a to-go box while dining out, which is much better than a full-fledged meltdown in McDonald's. Take two cars to an event so you have an escape plan if only one child is causing conflict. Margrey has been known to leave a full grocery cart at the store before checkout and take an unruly child home.

14. Always debrief as a couple or family. If there has been a particularly successful outing, debrief and celebrate with the kids.

You can have a giant list of ideas on pregaming, but you must start somewhere. Take action and pregame the one area that causes the most chaos in your life. Always plan, plan, and plan some more.

CHAPTER 10

CHOOSE YOUR MEDICAL TEAM WISELY

I am a doctor—it's a profession that may be considered
a special mission, a devotion. It calls for involvement, respect,
and willingness to help all other people.
—Ewa Kopacz, physician and former prime minister of Poland

MARGREY

You know it in every fiber of your body and in the deepest parts of your soul: you and your spouse are completely responsible for the care and nurture of your child. That doesn't mean you have to raise your child in a vacuum. You may be 100-percent responsible, but you are not in possession of 100 percent of the knowledge in the world and wisdom of the ages. Furthermore, you have limited perspective. You can't see everything that goes on. You need excellent, insightful, and dedicated professionals around you.

Every parent of a child like ours should have five teammates on the playing field at all times:

- Pediatrician
- Psychiatrist
- Pharmacist

- Psychologist
- Specialists (speech, physical and/or occupational therapists)

It's not enough to simply schedule appointments, drive your child to and from the offices, file insurance claims, and pay the bills. These professionals are your partners in care. They work for you and it is important for you to work with them.

Pediatrician

Medical stability is your primary concern. Before you can address psychology and behavior, you must address the body and medicines. Your pediatrician is your first care partner. He or she will be alongside you for all of the ear infections, cuts, broken bones, immunizations, school physicals, and adolescent angst you will face. Your pediatrician may be a good source of recommendations for other care providers and can watch out for symptoms, drug interactions, and how overall care is progressing. Based on your gut instinct and our suggestions, you'll find the right pediatrician to oversee your child's care. Your pediatrician should welcome input and suggestions from other specialty physicians.

We were blessed. Simply by luck, we bought the house next door to a pediatrician when our first child was just an infant. We've been neighbors for nearly thirty years, and on more than one occasion, Dr. Campbell dropped by the house on his way home from the office to take a look at one of the children. Blessings come in many forms, and some physicians still make house calls.

Psychiatrist

Children who look typical but are struggling with mental, psychological, learning, or developmental issues need the care of a medical doctor who specializes in brain chemistry. The brain is the key. All roads lead to and from the brain. The psychiatrist is trained to understand how behaviors stem from brain chemistry and can prescribe medicines to affect mood, hyperactivity, focus, and more. Like your pediatrician, this doctor understands normal physical, social, and psychological developmental milestones and where your child lies on that spectrum. The psychiatrist will first rule out any physical problems that may be causing or adding to the behavioral or mental health issues. Psychiatrists understand behavior—both normal and abnormal—and can look into your child's medications, confirming or adding to the regime.

During the first few appointments, the psychiatrist will evaluate your child and may prescribe medications. Over the coming weeks, he or she will watch your child's progress on the medications and listen to your observations. The effect of the medicines will vary, and it may take several weeks to determine a therapeutic dosage for your child. Be aware that these doctors will normally change only one medication at a time. Your role will be to observe your child closely so you can give the doctor exact feedback. Always write down the time of day of your observations and your child's behaviors to share with the psychiatrist.

Pharmacist

Build a relationship with your local pharmacist. You can deal with the pharmacy technicians more often than not for refills, but you should get to know the pharmacist and allow him or her to get to know your child. Be frank and honest yet respectful. If you have a solid relationship with your pharmacist, he or she will note subtle changes to medications and will closely observe your child. Often your pharmacist can share information with you that you can share with your psychiatrist.

Psychologist

Talk therapy or cognitive therapy can be very effective. The heavy lifting of your child's growth and maturation may come through the regular influence of your psychologist. Your choice and use of a psychologist have to come after your child is medically and pharmacologically stable. Once the medications are in place, counseling can be more effective. Financially speaking, once you are through the refinement of your child's medications, your time and the frequency of visits with the psychiatrist will probably decrease. Those finances and time can then be redirected toward visits to the psychologist. As mentioned previously, your church or community may have cost-effective alternatives in the area of counselors or psychologists.

Specialist

Your child might need a fifth member of their medical support team. Occupational or physical therapy, speech therapy, attachment therapy, or another type of care may become part of your regimen. Your child may have medical conditions that require a specialist. Select this care provider with the same precision as the other four. If your child needs special care, realize that the therapy or medical care will come with some homework assignments. The specialized care may be the key to unlocking the bigger picture for your child. Ask questions, and ask for demonstrations and/or hands-on training. Written instructions should be given to you. If not, ask for them. Be observant during therapy sessions, and don't talk or ask questions until the end of the session. Let the therapist do his or her work while you observe the technique and how he or she speaks to your child.

How to Choose Good Professionals

Research is your best friend. Before you make an appointment, ask friends, neighbors, family, and acquaintances about their doctors and the relationships they have. Ask people in your support group, in your Sunday school class, and at school events about their experiences with medical professionals that they utilize. Online reviews can be helpful, but they can also be the depository of resentful people who are never satisfied. Read them with your eyes open. When searching for a medical professional, consider these questions:

- What do you like about the doctor? Dislike?
- What challenges does your child have?
- How does the therapist interact with your child and with you?
- What else do you know about the doctor?
- Does the person who referred you use the same doctor?

After your research is complete and you believe you have a potential match, set an appointment. Remember, you're not marrying this professional. Your first appointment should feel more like a job interview than a first date; you are probing the doctor and observing him or her with your child. If you and your spouse can both attend the appointment, plan on it, and make every effort to be a parental team.

Always be on the lookout for professionals who might suit your child. We discovered one member of Dylan's medical team by accident. Dylan was about eight at the time and came with us to Heather's appointments. He wasn't making any progress with his current psychologist, and Heather's doctor shared a reception area with another psychologist. While waiting before appointments or sitting there during Heather's one-on-one time, we watched this other doctor take teenage clients for walks around the lake; we watched how he interacted with parents and how the boys responded to him. He was always upbeat and positive. We wanted this doctor on Dylan's team. During one of Heather's appointments, we introduced ourselves to this new psychologist and shared some of Dylan's story. He was open to setting an appointment, but we had some challenges because this doctor's office was already forty-five minutes away from our home, and Dylan was younger than his usual clientele.

We scheduled our first appointment with this new doctor, and Roy cleared his schedule. Our whole family was in attendance. After our first appointment, the doctor said, "I'll agree to work with Dylan even though he's younger than most of my clients. If I don't take him, he is likely to end up in jail or potentially dead before he's eighteen. He is bull-headed, hard-headed, every type of -headed you can be. I can tell you love him and want the best for him but are at the end of your rope."

During appointments, I watched the doctor teach Dylan. They took walks and had sessions in his office. I didn't do much at these appointments, just offered an occasional leading question, but I was so impressed by the doctor's manner and how Dylan responded. This was a successful choice, and this therapy and counseling was among the best Dylan ever experienced.

Your First Appointment

Before you go, prepare yourself. Make a list of the challenges and problems you face. Chart out any trends you've seen in your child's behavior.

This is a time to be totally honest with your physician, no matter how ugly your story appears.

Conveying to the physician trends or patterns in your child's behavior upon awakening, after school, during dinner, or at bedtime could alert the physician to an approach that may work well. Bring medications your child is currently taking. Write down a list of questions you have for the doctor; remember, you're interviewing him or her, not the other way around. I've never met a doctor, no matter how busy, who did not take the time to answer every question a patient or parent had written down before the appointment. This is a time to be totally honest with your physician, no matter how ugly your story appears. This is not a time to try and impress the physician with what a great family you have or what a wonderful parent you are. The physician is aware that you are there for help.

Also prepare your child. They should feel open enough to talk to the doctor in an age-appropriate manner. If your child has any questions, add them to your list to make sure you receive answers. Your child should clearly understand that the doctor is not an enemy or someone to fear; the doctor is here to help us, and we must tell the truth about our lives so the doctor has the best chance to help us. Tell your child that there will be no negative consequences or punishment for whatever they say to the doctor. Encourage honesty. Realize that your child may be testing you at the doctor's office. No matter what your child says, the doctor will easily see your child's behavior if your child is trying to push your buttons. Remember to relax your face and body—no reactions from you. Just look at the doctor, realize you are one of the adults in the room, and breathe.

During the appointment, remember again to be open and honest with the doctor about your family and your child. There is nothing this doctor hasn't heard or seen before. You are there for help. Your doctor can't help you if he or she doesn't know what the problem is. In many cases, it might be helpful to request medical records from your other doctors to be delivered before the appointment. The doctor may be able to review them prior to the appointment—even if just in the hallway—and will have them for reference during your appointment and afterward as he or she makes notes. Don't hesitate to ask your questions. It is easy to forget your questions when they are not written down.

The appointment doesn't end when the doctor leaves the room. You will have assignments or recommendations after you return home. Do what the doctor said, and see how his or her recommendations work.

Don't always judge the doctor based on a single member of his or her staff. Yes, you should expect good customer service from the team, but the most important thing is the doctor's care. If you are mistreated by any of the doctor's team, don't hesitate to bring it up to the doctor in private. His or her reaction to your input will tell you much about the doctor's philosophy of care. Your doctor should be vigilant that his or her entire team reflects his or her philosophy of care.

At one psychiatrist's appointment for Molly, I checked her in, got her settled in the reception area, and took a minute to visit the ladies' room. When I returned, the well-seasoned receptionist was scolding Molly. Every eye in the room was on either Molly, the receptionist, or me.

The woman leaned forward through the window and turned her laser-sharp gaze toward me. "Molly should sit down and behave."

I smiled and calmly reminded her, "Molly's behavior is the reason we see the doctor on a regular basis."

The whole room seemed to breathe. She quietly admitted, "I understand." Just as quickly as it started, it ended. I told the doctor about this, and our relationship with him and his employee continued smoothly for years.

What to Do at Subsequent Sessions

The pattern should repeat itself. In the process of doing homework, you'll have created a list of more questions and concerns. Write them down and bring them with you. If you've had interactions with other doctors in the meantime, make sure their records are forwarded to each other.

We recommend both parents take turns occasionally in taking your child to sessions. This will allow the professional to see how each of you responds and reacts to the child and what transpires during a session. Just as you and your spouse use your strengths and avoid your weaknesses, your child's physician will also work to your strengths.

Keep in mind, you're still not married to the professional at this point. You are going two or three times to observe patterns and also observe any change in your child. Your doctor may have put his or her best foot forward in the first meeting. Subsequent meetings will help your evaluations.

You are looking for a doctor who can maintain calmness and control no matter what happens. When Molly was six, I had a family emergency, and Roy took Molly to her psychiatrist appointment—we were making a critical change to her medication and couldn't miss this appointment. The doctor invited Roy back to her office and asked Molly to wait in the reception area while she talked privately with Roy. A couple of minutes later, they both returned to the reception area to bring Molly back to the office for the appointment. Molly ran ahead into the doctor's private office, innocently shut the door, and locked it. Roy and the doctor both tried to calmly talk Molly into opening the door. Partially due to Molly's comprehension skills, she did not even realize they wanted her to unlock the door. They struggled for long enough that Roy said to the doctor jokingly, "Do you have an extra key to your office? That may be something to have in the future."

"I'll make a note of that." The doctor maintained her cool through Molly's mistake and Roy's frustration. Roy said he and the doctor began to laugh about the situation. Finally, Molly unlocked the door, and the three ended up having a smooth session.

Evaluating Care Providers

After two or three sessions where both you and your spouse have been able to witness interactions, it's time to evaluate. Do you go from first dates to courting, or not? Here are questions to consider when deciding:

- What did your child think? Find out by asking open-ended questions such as, "What did you like best about Dr. Smith?" and, "How did you feel about your appointment?"
- Was your child able to be open and honest with the doctor? Were you?
- What does your gut say?
- Was the homework effective? Did you do the homework to the best of your ability?
- What small changes have you witnessed in your child's behavior or temperament?

Don't be afraid to pull the plug and look elsewhere. There was an instance where Dylan and his doctor were not a fit. We had a handful of appointments, and this professional was just too acquiescent to face off with Dylan's bull-headed personality. In essence, Dylan controlled every appointment by pushing and being manipulative. In the end, he just wasn't making progress like we felt he should. Remember, as a parent, you are in control of and responsible for your child's care. Lead the process; don't float along absentmindedly.

MARGREY

Medication Matters

We have always preferred doctors who prescribe conservatively and gradually but who aren't afraid to get creative if necessary. A conservative doctor will not want to shock the brain and the body with his or her prescriptions. The doctor will make his or her best evaluation and recommendation but initiate medications conservatively. Often a physician will insist that both parents be present when he or she is prescribing outside of the normal dosage range.

Molly needed Ritalin, but it had little effect on her initially. Her doctor eventually pushed the dose to a high—but not unprecedented—level. Her psychiatrist had to write letters on occasion to our insurance company to prove the medical necessity of her recommendations so they would continue to cover the monthly cost, but she did so proactively. Finally, she asked to meet with both Roy and me. She wanted to increase Molly's dosage of Ritalin beyond the recommended dosages. She reviewed all the pros and cons with us in great detail. She advised us of possible side effects. We made the informed decision to try the increased dosage. Molly's hyperactivity decreased markedly, and we had a child with more self-control and focus. Here are a couple of other suggestions regarding medications.

Watch. Get a good grip on side effects and watch for irregular behavior. Look for and log the side effects, along with the time of day. Keep a journal, which can double as a great place to write your list of questions for each doctor's appointment.

Lock Up Medicines. Prescriptions aren't anything to mess with, and you need to handle them responsibly. Buying a safe box with a combination or padlock and keeping the medicine bottles inside protects you and your child. If a safe box is impractical, keep medicines in the most strategic and safe area in your house, high and away from young children.

Stay on Top of Dosages and Refills. Write down the medications, dosages, and refill dates. Be sure to date your chart so that you can be aware of changes over time. Pictures of the pills can be helpful too. Generic medicines can often all look alike at first glance. If one parent is away and the other parent has to supervise medication distribution, the chart and pictures give confidence to the process.

Teach your child about each pill so they can start to be responsible and knowledgeable about their medication. When Molly was about twelve years old, we were at a pediatrician appointment and the doctor gave Molly a pill to take. Molly refused. "I am not going to take this. I didn't see the bottle. I'm not going to take it." The doctor tried to wriggle free from the dilemma. She found the bottle and showed it to her. That wasn't enough for Molly. "I won't take it. All my medicines come from Reeves-Sain Pharmacy." The doctor tried to convince Molly. "I'm your doctor. You can trust me. You've been coming to see me for years." Molly crossed her arms and stared at the doctor. A few minutes later, we left with a written prescription, drove eight blocks to Reeves-Sain Pharmacy, filled the prescription, and Molly took the pill without another word or complaint.

ROY

Trust but Verify. Watch your children take their medicine. Like Ronald Reagan said about Russia's nuclear disarmament: "Trust but verify."

Before heading to the dental office one morning, I saw Heather, who was in ninth grade at the time, standing next to the cabinet in the kitchen near the morning medications. Her pills were in a cup on the counter, as usual. She was hesitating for some reason, so I reminded her, "Take your meds, Heather."

As I walked away, I saw her deftly remove one of the pills from the cup and stick it in her waistband before knocking back the rest and chasing them with water. "Freeze!" I said as calmly as I could. After confronting her, recovering the pill, and having a short discussion, I asked Margrey to call the school immediately and ask for a visit with the administrator. I called my office manager and canceled the morning's appointments.

When we got to the school, we sat down with the school nurse, who was another member of Team Thompson. I said, "I don't think she's taking her medicines. We found several pills in her purse. Is she taking them at school? Is she getting supervised enough?"

The good news was that Heather wasn't selling them, and we found this was only a recent behavior. The administrator had also been concerned; she increased her inspection of the dispensing at school, and Heather got back on track.

One year, Molly went to a summer camp in the desert. When she came home, she would take her medicines and then open her mouth wide and roll her tongue around to let us see that no pills remained. She had brought this inspection behavior home from camp. Trust with verification works exceptionally well.

You must also assume responsibility for teaching your child about their need for medication and why it is necessary to their wellness to take it on schedule. Set a timer on your phone to remind yourself and your child. Teach about chronic illnesses. Let them realize that they can lead a healthy, functional life but that medication will probably be a part of their life forever. Since Margrey takes daily medication for a chronic illness of her own, she has been able to lead by example in responsible use of medication. She routinely discussed how she had to adapt and make the process of daily medication a permanent part of her life.

Beware of Generics. For most of us (and our bank accounts), generic medications are a godsend. From time to time, though, you might have a medical provider prescribe the name brand instead. Don't immediately slough this off. There's a reason behind the recommendation, and it's always about the effectiveness of the medication. Generic drugs can be effective, but they are not always exactly the same due to varying manufacturing processes. Trust your doctor. Many times, we started with a name-brand medication, and after a period of time, we would try the generic and evaluate the results on a daily basis. Some psychiatrists only prescribe name-brand medications, so be prepared for this policy.

MARGREY

Homework from the Doctor Matters

Unfortunately, you may never run out of problems for the psychologist or psychiatrist. And therefore, you will never run out of homework assignments from your doctors. The homework is only as effective as the time you put into it as a family. Realize that this home-work takes precedence over the North American lifestyle of constant activity. You have to let go of the expectations of

You have to let go of the expectations of the outside world.

the outside world. Your child will not thrive unless you're tackling these matters at home. You have to live your life by a different set of standards than the Joneses.

You don't have to be legalistic or perfect in your execution of homework. We weren't on task or on target each week, but it was always the goal. The key word is *consistency*. Just as when you brush and floss your teeth daily, sometimes you might miss a day. Don't beat yourself up if it didn't work one day. Start over the next day. This homework is the only way you can gain traction after your child is medically stable. The doctor's appointments don't change your child. The execution of the homework does. You become the therapist in this situation.

One week, our homework with Heather was to only make positive statements about her behavior. We were to catch her doing the right behaviors, even if for just a couple seconds at a time, and comment on them. The negative comments are so easy to find and to repeat. Our psychologist wanted us to work on capturing success. There were a few things we identified where praise was easy, like buckling her seatbelt and brushing her teeth, but the rest of Heather's life was chaotic. Take sitting at the dinner table. Heather wouldn't stay seated in her chair at dinner. So we had to watch for and cue ourselves to notice when her bottom was in the chair for ten seconds. It was difficult to go from saying, "Sit down," a hundred times each dinner to saying, "I love how you're sitting in your seat," once or twice per dinner.

It was hard homework for us, but we did it for two weeks, and it had an impact. We were able to see the results in ourselves and in Heather. We weren't successful all the time, and we weren't perfect in execution, but we inched along. Training yourself to ignore negative behaviors and focus on the positive is difficult to learn as an adult. Keep working, and always remember that your goal is progress, not perfection. Every time we saw just a little progress, we gained hope for the future. In our nightly debrief, we hugged each other and celebrated what most parents take for granted.

Homework must be a team effort. The assignments are not just for the spouse who attended the session. They are for both of you. When I returned from a therapy appointment, I would discuss it with the child and Roy together. Roy was always asking our children, "Tell me what happened at the doctor's office today. What are we going to try differently this week?" Open-ended questions like this will be more likely to engage your child in conversation. This empowers your child to have ownership of the appointment. Attempt to never ask a question that can be answered with a simple yes or no.

Marriage and the Medical Team

Typically, there is one spouse who is more efficient or skilled in dealing with medical professionals. That doesn't make this spouse stronger or weaker, just different. You are a team, and you are both responsible for your child's growth.

In our experience, the spouse who is more effective

- has more time available during business hours,
- sees the child in a variety of situations,
- can institute new rules quickly,
- can engage the physicians and therapists, and
- can communicate the appointments to the other spouse well.

Since Roy and I agreed that I was the primary parent in daytime responsibilities, I spearheaded the medical aspect of the children's lives. One doctor told us, "Many times the families don't know it, but I spend the first year working on the married couple to make sure they're stable before I begin working in earnest with the child. Roy, you are more analytical. You think through it. Margrey, you are more on-the-spot. You make decisions and run with them. You listen to each other and balance each other out. One of you isn't better than the other. You work together, and together that makes you an incredible team."

Your marriage relationship is more powerful in your child's life than any medicine. Your strong marriage gives your child the stability to grow and learn. Work together to build the best team for your child, communicate continuously and consistently about what the doctor wants you to do, and do your homework as a team, and you will be unstoppable.

When it comes to the medical team for your child, set the bar high and don't lower it. This journey is long and hard, and sometimes you may wish there was an open bar in the corner of your doctor's office. This kind of frustration is normal as a parent. Look for small rays of sunshine as you plow through the medical aspects of your child's care. You are appointed to care for the physical, emotional, educational, and psychological well-being of your child. Don't add just anyone to the team! Surround yourself with the best fit for you and your child, then move forward in confidence. Finally, remember, *you* are the expert on your child.

CHAPTER 11

WITHSTAND THE BULLIES

Sticks and stones may break our bones,
but words make us suck it up and get tougher.
—Roy Thompson

ROY

Bullies don't just pick on our children. When bullies target us as parents, their tactics are more refined than a shoulder shove in the school hallway or knocking the tray to the floor in the cafeteria, but we are bullied nonetheless with words, innuendo, and facial expressions. The closer the relationship, the more the words hurt. The words spoken by family members can hurt the most. We have heard it all. Have you heard remarks like these?

- "Why can't you control your child?"
- "If you would just discipline that girl, she would straighten up and fly right."
- "Why does your child keep looking at me like that?"
- "Can't you make these children behave?"
- "Why does he repeatedly make the same mistakes?

- "He could behave if he wanted to."
- "She's so loud!"

We've also seen it all. We bet you have too. The huffy-puffy woman who makes a swallowing noise, slightly raises her nose toward the ceiling, then pushes past you just fast enough that you know it was faster than necessary. The mother who tells her son he can't play with yours. The neighbor who sends your child home because she thinks your child has bad manners due to poor parenting. People who shake their heads as they walk past. These are the minor ways that strangers can express their slight objection to how you are attempting to control your child.

These incidents hurt because we continue to wrestle with fears and failures that have been present since the earliest days. You have an acute desire for your child to be typical and not be labeled abnormal. This desire will wax and wane but will be sharp at times. You have a desire to be an effective parent. We've felt it.

When a child is young, a mother doesn't know how they will turn out. She might not even know there are problems. She certainly doesn't know the severity of any diagnoses. Then, as the child grows up, matters become more complicated. Communication struggles ensue. The mother tries different medicines and dosages. The hormone wash of adolescence adds a level of complexity, confusion, and frustration, and the parenting tools she has used for years suddenly don't work. She will wrestle with constant questions throughout the child's life. Will they grow out of this? Is this adolescent rebellion or a deeper behavioral issue? What other diagnoses are coming? What might happen next? How can I ever control this child? Am I rearing a juvenile delinquent? Is this my fault? Is my spouse to blame? Could I be parenting different and better? And the ever-present thought: *I have no idea how to live through this.*

Your personal fears and internal arguments are enough to cause stress and sleepless nights. You feel vulnerable to criticism. You certainly don't need others' questions and insults added to the mix, yet they come anyway, uninvited and intrusive. The degree to which you fend off the bullies who confront you and your children is related to your personal strength, your resilience, your optimism, and your self-confidence. Your ability to trust the professionals around you—and more importantly, your ability to trust yourself—will help carry you through the hurtful words. Over the years, we have developed five habits that we rely on to navigate through the sharp words and actions of others. We are more immune than before, but we still put these habits into action every day:

1. Trust your professionals
2. Trust your gut
3. Support each other, and don't become a bully yourself
4. Acknowledge the ignorance
5. Time flies, so take the long view

Trust Your Professionals

That sarcastic woman at the grocery store and that man who shakes his head at church haven't spent hours managing your children. They haven't spent years reading, going to symposiums, sitting in classes, and working with countless children like yours. Those around you are looking at an out-of-focus snapshot of your child through their biased and inexperienced eyes. Your psychiatrist and psychologist are seeing a motion picture of your child's entire life in the context of their education and experience. The volume of their voices should be set on high, while everyone else's should be set on mute.

Listen to what they say about you and your relationship to your child. Accept the compliments and the exhortations. Take their positive words to heart. Write them down if you have to. Their voices should matter most. When the verbal or passive aggressive assault comes, remind yourself of what your professional team has said.

Be aware of where you are in your journey with your child. You can't work on every aspect of their growth and behavior at one time.

Your psychiatrist, psychologist, and pediatrician will have you working on a small swatch of life at any one time. Stay true to their homework, and let every comment outside of that scope bounce off you like a whiffle ball against Superman's chest.

Also know, however, that not all highly educated people will understand. Molly needed—and still needs for that matter—physical activity. She was never one to sit still. We registered her for a camp at our local college the summer she was twelve. She could run, jump, play games, and be active all day long. It was perfect for her. We disclosed Molly's diagnoses, and we were assured she was welcome and the staff was prepared.

On the first day, after the first two hours, the tenured college professor in charge of the camp telephoned and demanded that meet him on campus. She told me later her thoughts:

> He started in on me as soon as I walked into his office, and I wished you were beside me. "What were you thinking, allowing your child to come to this camp? I don't know what is wrong with your child, but she is not cut out for my program." He went on for several minutes. "Take your child. This is not the program for her!"
>
> Molly was glad to leave because the staff had been treating her this way all morning. I took her home and was broken-hearted for Molly. She quickly absorbed herself in playing with her cousin, but I went to my bedroom and cried for a long time. I thought to myself, *What am I up against when even educated, trained, well-read people can't cope with Molly?*

Even the "experts" can be bullies.

We've had mean teachers at times. We sat down with one during a parent-teacher conference; she plopped a trash bag in front of us and said, "Here are all the trinkets your daughter has brought to school lately.

Please take them home and make sure she doesn't bring any more stuff like this to school. I don't have time to be collecting all this stuff to return it to you."

We learned that if Molly brought *anything* to class, the teacher would crank up, get on her case, and confiscate any item.

"Take that hair bow out right now; you'll play with it."

"You've got two pencils. Hand me one; you'll play with it."

"Where did you get that? Put it in here. You'll be distracted by it."

Our school years typically ended with the teacher giving us the ceremonial plastic garbage bag. Of course, that bag was typically accompanied by the added insinuation of, *Here! This is all the stuff Molly snuck past you.* What did these teachers think? Was I going to strip search each of my children before getting them in the car? We were glad they were dressed in more than their pajamas most of the time. A trinket pirated out of the house was of minimal concern to us.

Find professionals you trust. Then trust the professionals you find—what they say, what they prescribe, and what they recommend. The best advice we received has carried us the farthest. One of our children's first psychiatrists told us, "You *will* have success. The problems of just one of your children would result in divorce for a couple most of the time. You've got three to parent. You've worked hard to get and keep yourselves healthy." That is the essence of this book: get yourself healthy, keep your marriage healthy, and your children will be healthy. It may take time to get everything in place, but it's worth it. Work together to bring your collective "A game" to the task of parenting. It takes two.

Trust Your Gut

Loving parents know their children best. A newborn's mom can hear only a few seconds of her baby crying and distinguish why the baby is crying. She can see the color of his face and know he will need a diaper change in a matter of minutes. A father of a preteen boy realizes his son will be angry before the son does. He understands when a groan is just a groan or when it is a bellwether of a coming storm.

Likewise, you know your child and their condition. You've seen and catalogued all of the precursors to a meltdown. You tell time by the attitude of your child based on the administration of the last dose of medication. You can analyze their tone of voice and know which way the emotional winds will blow. You have tools to calm your child that no one else knows and lightning reflexes to employ them. You know all of these things and internally celebrate your wisdom. You cannot get discouraged when a complete stranger with no knowledge or experience huffs, puffs, or rolls his or her eyes about your child.

Years ago, a female attorney friend of ours acted as a foster parent and transported young children between cities for different agencies. She told us that at one point she had a six-year-old child in the Nashville airport when the child had a true meltdown. She calmly sat down with her back against the wall, put the thrashing child between her legs, and wrapped her arms and legs around the child to physically restrain the out-of-control behavior.

Your gut instinct is one of your best sources of decision-making power.

As travelers walked by trying to ignore the scene, one woman slowed and gave a judgmental glance at our attorney friend. The young child, in her uncontrolled state, said to the passerby, "What are you looking at?" The lady quickly moved on. Outsiders rarely know what goes on in your life and can be unintentional bullies. Instead of having empathy for the parent who is doing the best possible at the moment, most people unintentionally look and pass judgment on the child and their out-of-control behavior and on the parent that seems unable to control their child.

Your gut instinct is one of your best sources of decision-making power. It's not perfect, but it has been forged in the fire of thousands of moments of tension and joy with your child and your spouse. It is informed by the professionals you trust and the learning you've absorbed. Your gut's reflexes are faster than Dr. Phil's or Dr. Laura's. You can trust it to lead you in the right direction when circumstances require a decision. So many of us, however, are afraid. We want to deliberate, check our instincts with another, or defer. We are afraid the consequences cooked up by our imaginations are too severe to make a gut call. Too often, these anxieties cause us to lapse into "paralysis by analysis" or freeze up altogether so that no decision is made. The wise parent is the one who trusts their gut and mutes the other voices.

Bullies can come in many forms and be unintentional. When Molly was in Brownies, they had a two-night retreat. Margrey was involved in her mother's recent hospitalization, but I was free and able to go, and I was agreeable to this, even with a predominantly female crowd. I was told and rightly agreed that I would need to stay in the counselor dorm where other parents and much younger children stayed. I warned that Molly needed her medications on time and that she takes time to settle down at night. Molly pleaded to stay with me. The next morning, with bleary eyes, Molly's counselor explained that Molly didn't settle down until nearly midnight. Inside I laughed at her naivety.

Later that day Molly was having difficulty with a task. The same and now frustrated counselor put her in a timeout and gave her an analytical paperwork task. I watched as Molly fell apart and the counselor continued to berate her. Even Brownie leaders have their limits. I let the event unfold and questioned internally whether I should intervene. That night Molly was moved to the counselor dorm. She slept soundly, and the other counselors slept better also. I questioned whether I had done the right thing as a parent earlier in the day but reassured myself that I did the best I could while making a split-second decision not to intervene on Molly's behalf. Don't live with regret or second-guess yourself when these situations face you. Trust that you did the best possible with the knowledge you had at the time.

There is a downside to acting from your gut: poor communication. Your gut doesn't carbon copy your professional team and your spouse when you use it. You must tell your mate what went down, your decisions, and the fallout every night when you debrief the day. It will also help you in the long run to keep your psychiatrists and other medical professionals in the loop. Sometimes, communicating about these incidents is hard. You might be second-guessed or contradicted. Your spouse and your professionals have the gift of distance, peace, and reflection. They were not in the hot seat, needing to make a decision. Hold loosely to your decision and be willing to learn from the situation for the next time. Your gut will thank you.

Support Each Other, and Don't Become a Bully Yourself

Children with developmental or psychological issues but no visible handicaps look like typical children. So others expect them to behave like typical children. Sometimes, we parents expect this too. Perhaps a series of good days lulls us into thinking things are better than reality. Sometimes a business trip gives one spouse distance from the daily rigors of care.

As mentioned before, we split one day's responsibility into two parts. Margrey was responsible for anything that occurred during work hours, and I was responsible in the evenings and overnight. For every story we share about Margrey calling me at work to ask me to come with her on behalf of a child, there are a hundred where she independently handled the situation with aplomb. Margrey has the self-confidence of a seasoned statesman. I tend to analyze a bit more and ask for more information.

When we would debrief in the evenings, she would tell me the stories and her decisions. My number-one job was to be her cheerleader, to support her decisions and help her know that her work on the frontlines was seen and appreciated. Sometimes, however, my questions hurt her. She felt I was questioning the wisdom of her decisions. Many times, she made decisions on my behalf and then expected me to enforce her decisions. Many times, I asked her not to paint me into a corner with one of her decisions. Debriefing could be a debate, but we always went to bed as friends. This is where you must have 100-percent trust and confidence that each of you has the best interest of your child and your marriage in mind.

Support also looks like a common front in the presence of your child. There will be times when a child asks you a question or for permission. You grant it, but your spouse disagrees. Supporting each other means demonstrating your togetherness in front of the child. You speak in one voice. What one parent says is undergirded by the other parent.

I'll never forget a subtle lesson we learned from our psychologist. She told us to stand side by side when talking to our children. For example, Margrey is washing vegetables for dinner at the sink, and I'm on the other side of the room, looking at today's mail. A child walks in and begins a conversation about going to a birthday party. It's easy to tell that the conversation will last longer than ten seconds, so I slowly walk over to Margrey and stand next to her at the sink as the three of us talk. In doing so, we are giving our child the visual cue that we are together and communicating on a subconscious level that the child cannot and does not come between husband and wife.

Sure, there will be times you disagree. Discuss those occasions calmly as adults in private. Don't tear down or disrespect your spouse in front of your child. If you feel a sense of urgency to address the issue, pull your spouse into privacy in such a way as to not signal disagreement. If in your private meeting you two decide to change the course of what was said, it is important that the same parent go back to the child and deliver the update. It's also important that this parent not throw the other parent "under the bus" in the process. Margrey and I are not perfect. We each have some tire-tread marks on our backs where the buses ran over us.

You two are in this together. It's an eternal three-legged race. Running is impossible unless you have your arms around each other, you match each other's stride, and you communicate.

Acknowledge the Ignorance

Years ago, Margrey started some internal coaching—some self-talk—after situations where others spoke harshly to the children or to her. Since she was the parent out in public with the children while I was at the office, she would simply think to herself, "God bless their itty-bitty hearts." We don't mean to be disrespectful of the insulter of our children. This person may have a big heart in other ways, but he or she has not considered his or her words. This person does not know what you know. You know all of the blessings that come alongside the hardships. You love your child. These individuals never saw you nurse your baby, sit up all night waiting for a fever to break, or watch in amazement as they read for the first time. The insulters weren't there for the epiphanies your child experienced when they learned a new tool for addressing their challenges. When it comes to your child, the insulter's heart is smaller than the Grinch's. You can pray it grows larger, but don't give the insulter too much credit. For that person, it was a passing comment forgotten by the time he or she cuts someone off in traffic a few minutes later. You know the truth. Acknowledge the ignorance and move on.

This is more difficult when the insulter is a member of your family and, no matter how much education and perspective you offer, the uneducated perspective takes years to turn around. You do not need permission for or approval of your parenting style from your family members. Over time we have found that family—given time and facts—can be the most understanding. However, information may never change another person's attitude. Acknowledge the ignorance and move on, but never, never write off a family relationship. Family is much too precious to wash out of your life. There are many other ways to continue to gain family understanding over time and maintain family relationships. None of your tools to educate will succeed if you've banished family from your life.

Time Flies, So Take the Long View

Tomorrow will come no matter what. It arrives faster than you realize. You can't be frozen by your fear and anxiety over what insulters might say or do. Their comments will be gone. You will still be side by side with your spouse, rearing your child and preserving your marriage.

When we feel anxious, experts tell us we run away (flee), dig our heels in (fight), or get stuck (freeze). The vast bulk of us neither fight nor flee. The majority of humans facing something difficult want life to be normal, so we freeze. Sometimes when we freeze up, we play back a recording of the insult or incident over and over again, causing us to become more and more frozen. We can even begin to let our imaginations run wild and make a catastrophe out of a small encounter.

We have to learn to respond well on these occasions. Most of the time, moving on and leaving the insulter in our wake is the best response. That means physically leaving the situation and mentally leaving the comments behind. "After all," as Scarlett O'Hara famously said in *Gone with the Wind*, "tomorrow is another day."

When we have died and our brothers and sisters are gone, we want our children to have healthy and active relationships with their cousins. That means we can't cut off our children's aunts and uncles just because they sometimes can be stubborn and lack insight into our children's worlds. Endure the pokes and prods now for the sake

Most of all, we felt humbled that God had entrusted our children to us.

of your children. Over time, family and friends come to appreciate and respect more deeply the trials you have endured in rearing your special needs child.

Near the end of her life, Margrey's mother came to live with us. She saw up close for the first time how much parenting we did on a daily basis. She saw how much energy it took to get ready for school and church, to do homework, to discipline the children, and to remain positive throughout the day. One night, she said to Margrey, "I never had to parent like you do. I told you things once and you always followed directions easily. You have to parent all the time!" Later, we asked my mother if she had worked hard raising me and my four siblings. Her answer was that her children just raised themselves, and she never had to spend as much time as we do rearing our children. When we heard comments like this, we felt exonerated. We felt gratified. Most of all, we felt humbled that God had entrusted our children to us. May you have that moment too.

You can't raise children in a vacuum, nor can they live in one. You and your child have got to learn to live with others. If it gets bad enough, you can drive your child to school every day instead of using the bus, withdraw your child from that activity, change churches, or move across town. Remember, you can't always freeze, and you can't always fight. You most often have to press through the friction and keep moving.

CHAPTER 12

ADVOCATE FOR YOUR CHILD

I will not stay silent so you can stay comfortable.
—*Anonymous*

MARGREY

During the Middle Ages, many communities had two ways of dealing with attacks from outside enemies. The ruler of a region lived in a castle with defenses—walls, a drawbridge, a moat, watchtowers, soldiers, and supplies. When an enemy approached, all of the citizens would rush to the castle and work with that ruler to protect the community. It was for this very reason residents provided a portion of their crops and paid high taxes. When under siege, the rular would send forth the other method of dealing with attacks: his emissary. This man was a diplomat, spoke many languages and dialects, was cool-headed, and negotiated well with both the enemy and neighboring allies. When it comes to parenting your special needs child, you and your spouse have to do both things: you've got to pull up the drawbridge, and you need to deal diplomatically with those outside the walls. We call this process "advocating."

You and your spouse are always ready to advocate for your child. There will rarely be a time when you don't have to be the voice of your child or, at the other end of the spectrum, defend them from harm. Advocating is the most valuable tool you possess but sometimes the most difficult one to master.

Before we had children, Roy and I had already spent years advocating on behalf of our patients. We wrote letters to our patients' physicians and to their insurance companies. We always fought insurance claims that were denied. It was not a new experience for us, but we never dreamed we would use that same skill as parents.

One of the most powerful forces in a marriage is the ability to stand united. This helps in your home when it is time to discipline a child or when there is an argument about who goes first when children are fighting over the TV. When one of our children would ask to attend an event or to hang out with a friend, one of us would give them an answer. If they weren't happy with the answer, we would invite them to go discuss the subject with the other parent. Often their response was, "Why should I waste my time and talk to Dad when he is just going to ask, What did your mom say? He is always going to agree with you." Our children learned that we stood united in their eyes. Many times, Roy and I would get together and discuss in private what the child was asking about and determine that maybe the child had a valid request and we should grant it. We simply told the children that we had heard them when they made the request, and we gave the request more thought and changed our minds. Sometimes the answer was still no.

When it comes to advocating for your child, if both parents are united in their beliefs and have confidence that they know what is best, they will meet with success over and over again. You can view advocacy as a team sport. One spouse may think more quickly on their feet and is the better spokesperson for your team. The other spouse may be a better researcher when it comes to interpreting the educational laws or may be more perceptive in figuring out how a school operates.

Negotiation Styles

We find that parents who advocate for their children fall into three negotiating styles: acquiescent, aggressive, and assertive. We would like your skills to grow toward the assertive style, but in order to grow, you need to be able to evaluate your current skills. Everyone should always be working on improving his or her advocacy skills. It is an ongoing art form and learning experience.

There are three parties to consider in your negotiations: you, the person or organization you are dealing with, and your child. Your utmost goal is an outcome that benefits your child. Depending on your style and the type of person you are dealing with, the outcome for each party will vary. You will always have your child's best interests at heart. The other party may not. They may be looking out for their own best interests. Your goal should be a win for you, a win for them, and primarily a win for your child.

Acquiescent. This is the easiest pattern of advocacy to fall into, especially when weary. Doctors, teachers, paraprofessionals, volunteers at church, and relatives all have their opinions and seem to never lack the will and desire to share them with you. Sometimes their arguments sound reasonable and logical. Yes, you need to trust your medical team, but we also tell you to trust your gut. Every time you acquiesce, or wimp out, in favor of someone else's opinion when yours is different, you're not truly advocating. Stand strong for your child. You are the expert. Don't ever forget that point.

If you tend to acquiesce, lean on your spouse and your medical team. Learn the phrase, "I'm not going to talk more about this with you until I discuss it with my spouse/medical team. I'm happy to talk about this again next week." Your acquiescence may create a loss for you, a win for the person you are dealing with, and an unknown outcome for your child.

Aggressive. It's also easy—too easy—to become aggressive. If you've been poked with a stick enough times, you're going to bare your teeth and growl a little bit. We all can recognize aggressive people. They are generally loud when talking and tend to invade your personal space; they may get in your face and be pushy. Many times, their chest is puffed out and they want to tower over you. They don't care who hears them or if they are interrupting others. Generally, there is no negotiation with this individual. It is their way or the highway. You may be aggressive because you are at the end of your rope, or you may just be too tired to cope with another dilemma. You may have been hurt too many times to count. If you're aggressive, you may not have the diplomacy skills you need. Most times you won't be heard, or those you are negotiating with will push back just because they don't like your style. In this case, everyone loses—you, the person you're negotiating with, and your child.

Assertive. Being assertive is the most balanced of all three categories, in our opinion. The assertive parent is understanding and has an agenda in mind but has grace under fire. The assertive parent understands that there may be more facts at hand than they understand and seeks to understand before presenting their side of things. When I first started my physical therapy business in my midtwenties, I was a tiger and a hothead when I felt I was right about some matter. My attorney, a nice, easy-talking Southern gentleman, sat me down one day and told me how we were going to negotiate a deal I was working on. He believed I could get the deal I wanted if I played the game his way. His way was the old adage, "You catch more flies with honey than with vinegar." I agreed to do the negotiation his way, and I walked away with what I desired. I never forgot the lesson, and I worked on imitating his style every chance I got.

The assertive parent doesn't let go when things get tough but at the same time doesn't rip flesh and draw blood. Winston Churchill once said, "The nose of the bulldog is slanted backwards so he can continue to breathe without letting go." Be a bulldog for your children!

For wives, it can be difficult to be assertive. Ladies, don't worry if people label you aggressive when you are only being assertive. This happens often in our current society. Stay focused on your skills. Stay focused on your child. This is about your child, not you.

In summary, no matter what your style of diplomacy, remember to persevere day after day and year after year. Your child needs you to develop these skills so they can survive in this world. Never give up or give in.

Advocating within the School System

The children's bus driver once called to confront us about our kids' behavior. Roy told him, "Tell me what you expect of my kids, and I'll do everything I can to get them to obey."

The driver barked, "I want them to sit their butts down on their seats and push their backs against the seat. They shouldn't get up the entire ride."

Roy replied, "Thank you. I'll coach them on that and help out." That night, he and I arranged a few kitchen chairs to pretend we were riding the bus. I was the bus driver and welcomed them on. After a few times, they got the message: we expected them to respect the bus driver's request.

After we were done, Heather said, "You don't understand. The bus driver is mean to Molly."

A few days later, the driver called again. "Your kids had their hands in the air the entire route. And they got other kids to raise their hands too. I can't drive with all of those hands in the air."

Roy asked, "Did they sit in their seats with their backs against the seats?"

"What? Uh, yeah . . . yes, they did."

"Well, the other day, you didn't mention anything about hands."

The bus driver exclaimed, "I can't go into every detail of what your kids can and can't do!"

"If you can't give me specifics, I can't coach them on what you need," Roy said.

He complained a little bit longer while Roy struggled to stay calm, and then we moved to an alternative solution. "Well, what if we got a seatbelt installed on the front row and have Molly sit there?"

"I can't have her up there near me," he responded. "She talks all the time! She acts like one of those kids from the wrong side of the tracks."

"So you want her to be silent in addition to sitting still the entire time and not raising her hands?" Then I heard Roy say something he shouldn't have. "Why don't we just build a box and drag her behind the bus?" The phone call ended in a stalemate.

I called the director of special education for the district, explained the challenge, and asked for his advice. He called the manager of school transportation, who showed up early one morning at the terminal and then climbed on our children's bus for a ride-along.

That afternoon, the transportation manager called and said, "I don't see your children acting any differently from most of the other children on the bus." He shared some observations, then added, "But we are going to install a seatbelt on the front row and put Molly there. She won't be able to bump his seat or anything. I'm also going to ride along from time to time." We never had another problem.

To work effectively with school administrators, you must become an expert on your child's diagnosis. The diagnosis that our three children had in common was ADHD. This is where our area of expertise is strongest. Due to Molly's speech and language delays, plus her auditory dilemmas, we had to educate ourselves in another area of disability and how the school system could accommodate her disabilities. Heather was dyslexic, so we had to become creative in finding the best ways for her to gain information. Whatever your child's special diagnosis, one or both parents need to gain a sound understanding of that condition. Each of our children required some special knowledge on our part.

No one is ever going to be as knowledgeable about your child as you, regardless of your educational background.

Being an advocate for your child is an extremely important skill to develop. No one is ever going to be as knowledgeable about your child as you, regardless of your educational background. Being an advocate doesn't mean that you have to enter into a fist fight with every principal or bus driver, but it does mean that you need to understand the laws that are written to provide your child an education in our country. Once you understand the law, then you have to become a skilled negotiator. You will not win every fight, and you need to decide which battles to fight and win.

The three laws that may affect your child are

- the Rehabilitation Act of 1973 (RA),
- the Individuals with Disabilities Education Act (IDEA), and
- the Americans with Disabilities Act of 1990 (ADA).

There are numerous resources on the internet regarding the above-mentioned laws. Many parents have created blogs to discuss their child's progress at school or medical conditions; some are just sharing their knowledge. A great website when I needed some legal information was www.wrightslaw.com. They also offer webinars and seminars on advocating for children. I attended one of their seminars and purchased several of their books. Most of what I know about IDEA came from this resource. These two attorneys have dedicated their careers to advocating for children. Since I had a more flexible schedule and more free time to conduct research and read, we decided that I had to become the legal specialist of the family. I am not qualified to speak as an attorney, but below is my understanding of each law.

The ADA and RA are civil rights statutes that prevent discrimination but do not provide funds for the activities mandated by them. The IDEA, enacted in 2004, and the special education regulations include specific requirements for IEPs of children whose behavior impedes their learning or the learning of other children, including training teachers to use positive behavioral interventions and strategies. Originally IDEA covered children beginning at age three. Part C of IDEA is program for infants and toddlers with disabilities and is a federal grant program that assists states in operating a comprehensive statewide program of early intervention services for infants and toddlers with disabilities, ages birth through age 2 years, and their families. Part C was enacted in October, 2011. The IEP (Individualized Education Plan) is the centerpiece of the IDEA. It is a document that you develop along with the special education team at your school. It will clearly outline the special education services your child will be receiving, plus any related services, like speech therapy or adaptive equipment.

Think of the IEP as a legal contract between the parents of the special needs child and the school system. The IEP is a detailed description of exactly what steps the school *must* take in order to provide your child a "free and appropriate public education." There are many definitions of that word *appropriate*, and this is where your negotiating skills will be necessary.

There is an IEP team at your child's school. This is a team of educators plus the parents. The classroom teacher, the special education teacher, and a representative of the local school or educational district must be present. There must always be personnel, provided by the school, who can interpret the results of any tests conducted on your child. Once Molly had an audiological exam for her diagnosis of CAPD (central auditory processing disorder), I asked if the audiologist who evaluated Molly could be invited to the IEP meeting.

> *There must always be personnel, provided by the school, who can interpret the results of any tests conducted on your child.*

The answer by the district special education director was a blatant no. The school didn't want to pay for her time to attend the meeting. When it came time to review the audiological evaluation, I asked one simple question during that meeting, which was being recorded: "Excuse me, who in this meeting is qualified to interpret and explain the audiological evaluation to Dr. Thompson and me?" Every head around the table went down, and there was no eye contact. Finally, the special education director mumbled that I had requested an audiologist and she had refused me. This was a clear violation of the IDEA, or our child's rights, and it was quickly corrected by scheduling a conference call with the audiologist. She asked if we could meet the following week and for the conference call. My answer was yes. This is a perfect example of what can happen if you are not well informed.

Always attend the IEP meeting highly prepared. It is like presenting your case in court. First, decide what your child needs. Write it down; let friends who know your child or other educators review your list. Doctors and psychologists will help you with this list. Take all your documents and reports. You keep the originals, but make a copy for the school system. Most important, don't go alone to this meeting. Both parents need to be present. You can invite people as you want for support or to help listen to the ideas of the school. Just be polite and tell the principal or special education instructor whom you are bringing. It is a common practice for the school system to load their side of the table with educators and have you sit by yourself on the other side of the table. Parents can easily get bombarded or overwhelmed and then acquiesce. Sometimes that could be the school's plan. Don't get yourself in that situation.

You can always ask for a short break during these meetings. You can ask to excuse yourself to the hallways to talk in private with your spouse or other attendees. If you want to speak quietly to your spouse, just pick up your legal tablet and place it in front of your faces and talk. This is done in legal meetings all the time. You see NFL coaches do this on the sidelines at every football game. You are in the middle of negotiations, and you are positioning yourself to win for your child. You are actively

You are actively advocating for your child. If you don't do this task, ask yourself, who will?

advocating for your child. If you don't do this task, ask yourself, who will? The answer is no one except a parent who loves his or her child!

About a month before the M-team (multidisciplinary team) meeting, ask the special education teacher for books, lists, or examples of possible goals with benchmarks for you to read and study ahead of time. This is the meeting where the IEP will be created. Make a list of the top three hurdles or concerns you have that you feel will be a roadblock to your child's success in the classroom. At the M-team meeting, the group will decide on major goals and will create benchmarks by which your child's progress will be judged. Your child will probably have several goals in their IEP.

Meet with the principal in April or May of the year before your child starts school in the fall. Discuss your child's disabilities and what kind of teacher would work best for your child. I never requested any particular teacher. The principal and I would discuss my child's strengths and weaknesses. We would discuss my concerns for my child. I always let the principal choose the best teacher for my child. One of my children worked best with the highly organized teacher who started with chapter 1 and proceeded through the book, as opposed to skipping around in the book. It sounds simple, but it was what worked for my child.

Focus on your child's specific difficulties when creating the IEP:

- Reading, spelling, and math
- Developmental milestones (don't forget social skills milestones!)
- Difficulties with processing or retaining information
- Trouble with sleeping or eating
- Trouble with paying attention or loss of focus
- Inappropriate behavior (just be open and honest here)
- Medical issues

In the IEP process, don't be surprised to hear the following statements (sometimes I wondered if there was a script for the educators, because I heard the same words from different teachers regarding a different child in a different school year so often!):

- Your assessment is incorrect.
- I'm sorry, Mrs. Thompson, the law doesn't say that.
- I will not agree to that request.
- Maybe they do that in Nashville, but we don't do it here.
- We don't provide that service.
- That is not our policy.
- It won't be fair to other children who may not get that service.

When you get these kinds of comments, make statements and ask questions like these:

- "Tell me more."
- "Explain to me your thinking behind that decision."
- "Can you show me in the law where it says that?"

Be prepared for vague answers. Most teachers and principals, although familiar with the law, are not experts. They rely on their central office for that information. The central office does not see your child, and it only represents the school system. Remember that it's a good idea to record these meetings so you have a confirmation of what was said.

Pay close attention to what is written on an IEP. Do not sign it until you can take it home and read it in a relaxed mode. It is absolutely necessary for you to state your position clearly on the IEP. Legal words are not necessary. Just write a complete sentence stating your concerns or problems. Remember, *do not be intimidated!* You are in control. An IEP has to be in place before the school year begins. This is the school's responsibility. Help them out by scheduling yours early if you think it may take several times to meet with the team in order to plan your child's IEP. You may request an IEP meeting at any time during the school year. Type or write a letter requesting the date and time of a meeting. Keep a copy of everything you send to the school.

Pay close attention to what is written on an IEP. Do not sign it until you can take it home and read it in a relaxed mode. Remember, do not be intimidated!

Remember, this is a legal relationship with the school system from day one. Do everything in writing. If your requests are in letter form, then your letter will get more attention and be remembered. Keep a journal of every conversation and use a three-ring binder to keep track of every document. Write the date on every document. If I hand-delivered a letter to the office, on my copy of the letter, I would write on the top of the page, "Hand-delivered to Ms. Smith, principal at John Paul School, on 2/15/1998 at 2:00 p.m." Your initials are necessary. If you ever have to recruit legal assistance, then you are fully prepared.

I recommend that you record each meeting. Let the school system know this ahead of time, because they will record the meeting also, through their own device. This is standard practice. You are not being weird if you make this request. Remember, these are legal negotiations. You are the *expert* when there is discussion of your child. Your position as the parent is to see that the school system adheres to the IEP. When a deviation from the plan surfaces, your role is to notify the school and realign their actions with the IEP.

You will typically be worried, overwhelmed, and emotionally upset at the idea of having to have an IEP meeting. This is normal. These meetings are stressful. Roy hated having an IEP meeting and then having to go back to the office to treat patients. We had our meetings end just before lunch so that he had time to decompress and get back into his doctor mode and out of parent mode before restarting his afternoon patients. It is draining and exhausting, and if you have any of these feelings, then you are absolutely normal. Always allow plenty of time on your schedule. Don't plan events or activities afterward. Make arrangements ahead of time so that your only focus is the IEP meeting.

One of the greatest gifts that we gave all three of our children is a regular high school diploma. No one received a special education diploma. A special education diploma is appropriate for kids with certain disabilities, but a high school diploma opens so many more doors for future employment. Dylan joined the Army and is now in college. Heather went to college for two years and lives and works independently in another state. Molly is in a residential program, working on her job skills so she can work part-time. Working with the school system throughout their educational lives has been critical to their successes.

You may have never thought you would act like an attorney or have to actually read the IDEA. You may have never envisioned that you would be going head to head with the school board on behalf of your child. We learned that the IDEA carries great power for the child with disabilities. We came to understand how their rights to a free and appropriate education are protected. Most importantly, we came to realize that we were the only ones that would truly fight for our children's rights. Be thankful that individuals in the past had the foresight to protect your child now. Individuals fought in Congress on your behalf years ago. Our democracy is precious, so get a copy of the law and read it several times, until you know it backward and forward. You will get through the educational maze with success for you and your child.

CHAPTER 13

DISCIPLINE IN LOVE

Don't worry that your children never listen to you;
worry that they are always watching you.
—*Robert Fulghum, author*

MARGREY

As your child grows up, you will constantly wrestle with reality. You don't know where the child will end up; you won't know at age five or ten or sometimes even at age twenty. You want your child to be typical and not be labeled abnormal. You will struggle with letting go of or adapting your expectations and dreams. How do you move your child along the path?

The word *discipline* is often used as a synonym for *punishment*. A child breaks a rule and must be punished for what happened. In reality, discipline is far more about correcting the wrong behavior or attitude and training the child in the correct way. With our children, discipline is a marathon and not a sprint.

You do not discipline a child in a vacuum. Many parenting books we've read speak to one parent as if the other parent isn't in the home or in the picture. In reality, you and your spouse have to present a common and consistent front to your children in order for them to correct wrong behaviors and attitudes and learn to practice the right ones. Parenting as a married couple isn't like the television shows of a bygone era either. Often the homemaker would say when a child got out of line, "Just wait till your father gets home." The orchestra would then play ominous music, and the camera would zoom in on the face of a frightened child. This technique didn't work in real life then and doesn't work in real life now. You can't routinely pass off discipline from one parent to another. This will begin to undermine the authority of the parent passing off the discipline. You must also avoid the critical mistake of debating discipline techniques in front of your child. You are a team.

Getting Started

Roy and I came into marriage from similar backgrounds. Discipline methods were not bones of contention for us. We both knew that spanking, removing privileges, and time-outs were all viable tools, and we were open to discover others. In sharing experiences with other couples, we've learned that there are many arguments that center on what form of discipline to use with their children. Where are you and your spouse? Have you ever discussed how you will discipline your child? What worked for you as children?? What scared you or scarred you? Take the time to put your heads together about this issue. Your child won't see a common front if you aren't in agreement on how to discipline and when to discipline.

Discipline is a tricky topic and very personal. Your experience with childhood discipline might be vastly different from ours. Yours may be vastly different from your spouse's. I remember one Sunday sitting on the side of the tub in my underwear, waiting for my dad to come in and give me a spanking for having wiggled around too much at church. Roy remembers being spanked by both hand and belt, being disciplined with a switch from a bush in his backyard, and even being paddled at school. Neither Roy nor I are scarred from our childhood discipline, and we actually can't argue that we probably deserved some type of punishment. Your story might include abuse or neglect. This is not the type of discipline we are discussing. We encourage you and your spouse to discuss your childhood discipline and come to terms with the limits you will set in your family. The common front is that important, and until you achieve this agreement, your discipline will not work.

The Hardest Part

As you begin to work together on consistent discipline, you may run into the same problem Roy and I have experienced. We were home in the mornings when the children were school-aged, so we could cooperate on any discipline issues that happened during those hours. When the children arrived home from school, I was at home and Roy was at work. I was on my own and made many decisions alone. When Roy got home in the evenings, he often took the lead until bedtime.

At times, I have come up with a discipline strategy or technique and said, "Now, Roy, you have to follow it through." For example, I was home once when Dylan crossed the line. I grounded him from TV (now we would say "screen time for all mobile devices") for a week. However, I expected that Roy would be the one who had to supervise Dylan to make sure he was not watching TV.

In situations like this, Roy would say to me, "Wait a minute. You've loaded me down with something I can't do." I realized that since Roy was not at home during the workdays, he could not be the one making sure Dylan wasn't sneaking off watching TV. Roy was right. I was creating problems he couldn't solve and that had to be enforced by me. We've had to work over the years to each help the other spouse be effective in discipline.

ROY

Discipline Is Different for Our Children

Children with developmental, psychological, and educational challenges don't respond to discipline techniques the way many typical children do.

How we discipline is as important as disciplining as a team. Many special needs children just don't get it; they don't understand as well when they've been in trouble and discipline is required.

For example, natural consequences may not work like you expect. Our children did not have the executive-level thinking and reasoning skills to undergo a natural consequence and make changes for the next time. They also sometimes couldn't apply lessons learned from one situation to another.

For example, let's consider wearing a coat to play outside when it's forty degrees and cloudy. Let's assume that Heather doesn't yet pay attention to the weather and doesn't pay attention to what other children are wearing outside. She runs outside in just her short-sleeved top. An hour later, she returns for dinner, and she is very cold and complaining about not wearing a coat. The next day, the weather is roughly the same, but she makes the same mistake. Children with the challenges ours have don't always connect the dots. Therefore, natural consequences take many years to learn.

Children with developmental, psychological, and educational challenges don't respond to discipline techniques the way many typical children do.

As a teenager, Molly had Beanie Babies. She kept making bad deal after bad deal when trading her Beanie Babies but didn't have the processing skills to learn from her decisions. She often had buyer's remorse about the trades but couldn't correct her thinking and acting. Once she earned a little money, she experienced the same type of buyer's remorse with many purchases. Now, in her midtwenties, she's finally gotten the concept and thinks on a deeper level. She called recently and told me that she thought through her purchase of a phone case and doesn't have any buyer's remorse. Natural consequences worked, but about ten years later than we had hoped.

Concrete Discipline

Our children needed discipline communicated in three different ways:

- See the discipline
- Hear the discipline
- Feel the discipline

See the Discipline. A chart showing the disciplines of the day was a permanent fixture in our kitchen. On any given day, one of our children may be in hot water. The chart reminded all of us which discipline had been assigned. The chart was there for both Margrey and I to see daily, so we were in the know. If I forgot to tell her about Dylan losing television privileges or Heather being grounded for the night, the chart held the information. The chart was a constant reminder to our children about where they stood—and a warning to not get in trouble again.

On and off over the years, we used a token system for behavior modification. The children earned tokens for positive behavior, and tokens were lost for negative acts. Over time we found that system was too complex and time-consuming for our family of three children, yet it might work for yours.

It is said that you need to give ten positive comments for every corrective comment you make. When you have children constantly making poor choices, this becomes overwhelming to parents and demoralizing to the children. Often, we ignored the bad behavior and chose our battles carefully.

Seeing the discipline can come in a different format as well. When Dylan was in first grade, his teacher called me on a Monday afternoon. She relayed why Dylan was coming home with a hole in the front of his shirt: The class had been working with scissors that morning, and Dylan looked up at his teacher, took his scissors, and brazenly cut a small hole in his shirt. She was devastated by his behavior and wasn't sure how to handle it. My brain works fast, and I had the perfect discipline. When I arrived home, I casually took Dylan to the bathroom and stood him on the vanity in front of a large mirror. I stated, "You like cutting your clothes?" Dylan did not answer me, as I anticipated. "Since you enjoy having a hole in your shirt, let's try this." I took a pair of scissors and cut three or four holes in his already ruined shirt, all while his eyes were bugging wider. "This will be your shirt to wear the rest of this week." He did wear it, and I informed his teacher that he was going to wear it all week. Dylan wore his jacket all day every day that week to cover that shirt. His teacher said he was sweating the whole time.

Dylan never cut his clothes again, but later in the year, in an even more brazen way, he made eye contact with the same teacher and took a small nip at his hair. His teacher called me again and knew what his discipline would be. She said that when she saw him cutting a piece of his hair, she was thinking, *Please, please don't cut your hair! I know your Dad, and I know what you will look like tomorrow.*

As she expected, I took a few more chops at his hair that evening on the same vanity. It took months for his hair to grow out. Not only did Dylan never cut his hair again, he never cut *anything* intentionally again. Discipline sometimes must be dramatic to a tough child. This is never done to embarrass or humiliate the child but to reinforce that you are in charge and will not tolerate certain behaviors.

Hear the Discipline. We discovered the hard way that our children needed to be reminded of their discipline on a regular basis. If Molly lost swimming privileges for three days, she needed to hear that discipline in the morning before school, after arriving home from school, and probably at least once more in the evening. Speaking about the discipline also gave us an opportunity to praise positive behavior, and it was a reminder to the other children that we were keeping track.

Feel the Discipline. Dylan's Sunday school often handed out candy bars as prizes. Dylan discovered where they stashed the chocolate and became a cat burglar. He wasn't stealthy enough, and he got caught. He felt the discipline in his wallet. For every chocolate bar he stole, he had to return four to the teacher. He had to do extra chores around the house at a rate of twenty-five cents per hour to earn the money to pay for the chocolate. As a final discipline, he had to look the teacher in the eyes and apologize.

MARGREY

Creative Discipline

In order for your child to see, hear, and feel the discipline, you will need to be creative. Some of you may not *feel* creative; you're not alone. So many nights, I cried in Roy's arms in prayer, feeling like the worst mom in the universe. I didn't know how I could get through another twenty-four hours with our children. I felt empty and out of ideas. By morning, I found new ideas that sustained me for another day or two. Pray and be honest with your spouse; I believe you'll find the creative ideas you need too.

Molly once earned the privilege to attend a concert. Once concert tickets are purchased, it's hard to just chuck them into the garbage when your child loses control, and with Molly, the anxiety around potentially losing the concert would only create more bad behavior. It was a vicious cycle leading only to bad results. So we came up with the idea that the concert was a sure thing and wouldn't go away. We decided to add a bonus to the concert evening as incentive for staying on track. We would stay in Nashville the night of the concert, which was a bonus for me too, so I didn't have to drive home so late after the concert. We also decided that if Molly stayed on track, she would get a concert tour T-shirt, a light stick, or dinner out before the concert. We put these incentives on a poster, and starting a month prior to the concert, if she displayed great behavior, she received more concert bonuses. Leading up to the concert, poor behaviors lost her more of the special privileges, but the concert was always a guarantee. We made sure there was always room for success. This plan worked for all of us.

Dylan began going to private school when he was in seventh grade. After two years of him getting Cs and Ds, we decided something had to be done. One Saturday I took Dylan for a drive; we pulled up in front of the local public high school, and I stopped the car.

"Why are we here?" Dylan asked.

"I thought you would like to see where you'll be going to school next year if your grades don't improve."

We discussed grades, attitude, and his future for a few minutes, and then I drove home. There was no big lecture; just facts. Dylan didn't improve his grades, and we sent him to public school for the remainder of high school. In the end, that was a great decision for Dylan. He flourished at public school. He participated in multiple extracurricular clubs and sports, his grades jumped dramatically, he was less stressed, *we* were less stressed, and there is no tuition in public school. Dylan literally saw, heard, and experienced this discipline.

Consistent Discipline

Discipline for both typical children and children with special needs will require endurance. You must stay the course, be encouraging, be a teammate with your child, make it fun at times, and keep at it. Don't give up if your child doesn't get it the first time. Roy reminds his patients every day to brush and floss their teeth so they keep their gums healthy, avoid cavities, and keep the plaque off for a beautiful and healthy smile. A dentist reminds patients of these tasks at each visit. Expecting a patient to succeed at this with only one reminder is as unreasonable as expecting your child to correct unwanted behavior with a cursory comment. Brushing teeth once is not enough; it's a twice-daily discipline. In order for discipline to take effect in your child's life, it must be consistent. You must be vigilant to make sure that your child is following the rules set forth in their discipline.

Evaluate What's Working

Part of endurance and vigilance is evaluating how well your discipline works. During a daily debrief, talk about one of your discipline techniques with your spouse. It's pretty obvious when discipline isn't working. We believed that if we had to suffer through a child's discipline more than the child, then it wasn't working.

Here are seven questions for every discipline:

1. How well did we communicate it to our child?
2. How well did I communicate it to my spouse?
3. How well did we enforce it?
4. Did medication play a role in how well this idea worked?
5. At what point in the course of the discipline did our child's behavior and attitude turn? How much?
6. How would we improve it for another use?
7. Do you think it would work for one of our other children? Why or why not?

Our professional training and years of experience have taught us the value of peer review of procedures. In the middle of a discipline, you may not be able to see what's going on. You're reminding your child, saying no, and attempting positive reinforcement yet still counting the hours or days until the discipline is over. By discussing it with your spouse at the conclusion of the discipline or in your evening debrief, you will gain another perspective and be able to think critically about what worked and what didn't. These evaluations are often good for coming up with new ideas too.

ROY

Extraordinary Measures

When Dylan was fourteen, he copped an attitude and got mouthy. It wasn't the first time, but this time it was more severe. There was a hardness to his face and words. He was out of school for summer and decided that he wouldn't do any work around the house. He was going to sit around in his room all day, ignore his chores, and just be lazy.

Margrey responded, "That's unacceptable. If you're not going to work, then you don't get to enjoy air conditioning. You can spend all day in the garage." There was an old couch in the garage, and Dylan laid around on it. Margrey served his meals there. Dylan was stubborn enough that he sat in the garage the entire day, through terribly hot weather, doing nothing.

The next day, Dylan doubled down. "I'm not doing anything, and I'm not staying in this garage."

Margrey called me at the office, and we discussed sending Dylan to a program that could better deal with his issues—something like a wilderness program or boot camp. There are many kinds with different philosophies that we had looked into previously, as we thought we might be headed in this direction with Dylan. We had figured out which one we might use if the situation ever called for it; we needed it now.

The next forty-eight hours after we chose a program are a blur in my memory. Dylan boarded the airplane for the nine-week program without any resistance, although he was mouthy and rude right up until departure. He said to us, "It's not like I'm going to boot camp." We sent Dylan with nothing—no change of clothes, no toothbrush, absolutely nothing. It broke our hearts to do this, but we knew that trouble was ahead if we didn't do something to change his attitude. At camp, Dylan had to hike eight to ten miles a day, he had to surrender his shoes at nighttime, and he needed permission to use the restroom. Campers had to ration their food each week to make it last, and they learned a different way of interacting with adults. At parents weekend, Dylan was quiet, only responded when spoken to, and mostly kept his eyes directed toward the ground. His sarcasm had transformed into subservience for the time being.

During his stay, we received a call that Dylan had been in a fist fight. The boy he fought was taller and older. Their fellow campers had gotten tired of these two kids arguing, so in the middle of the night, they secretly cordoned off an area and told the two to fight it out. The counselors discovered them fighting, and for several weeks, the boys slept serpentine, head to toe, with counselors dispersed between them. These wilderness programs have their own form of discipline. It was scary to sign papers giving health care power of attorney to a stranger and promising to cover the cost for law enforcement if they had to chase down a runaway child.

As a parent, you must make tough decisions when extreme discipline is needed.

Dylan came home a different young man, but he returned to the same environment, where the relationships and conflicts hadn't changed. He was still hard-headed, but the program was transformative and became a defining moment in our relationship with him. We don't know where Dylan would be—or where our relationship with him would be—had it not been for his time in the desert.

We used a similar program for Molly. From the age of ten to fourteen she suffered from severe anxiety. Her anxiety kept her homebound; she was afraid of leaving the house alone. Her psychiatrist tweaked her medication, and suddenly one day her anxiety disappeared. Soon after, she announced she was going to the store, hopped on her bicycle, and headed out. With her independence, she developed some resistance to parenting. She would often challenge us by saying, "You'll have to make me do that." She was never physically violent, but she was verbally belligerent.

We sent her to a different program, one designed for maximum physical activity. Molly needed to go to bed exhausted every day, or she would wear out anyone and everyone around her. At her program, she got fit. She did not see a Coca-Cola for nine weeks, and she had to deal with her noncompliant behaviors.

We visited Molly and Dylan during their programs on parents weekends. At each weekend program, we noticed that other parents and children were struggling in different ways, and they seemed to be in difficult places. We saw single parents struggling with recalcitrant children. We saw adolescents with different (not worse, just different) issues. We saw married couples that were divided; we saw married couples where only one parent came to visit; we saw married couples that obviously had issues of their own. Parenting a special needs child with behavioral issues is difficult even with two healthy parents; it is overwhelming and exhausting with a single parent.

When we discuss these life- and sanity-saving programs with other parents, they have two major objections. First, they are blinded by the dollar signs. We had to swallow the idea of expense too, but we applied this logic to our situation: At the time, we felt that Dylan and Molly were not college-bound. We felt the money we had planned to spend on college would be better spent on programs to help them face their issues and grow into self-reliant adults. We knew if they turned out to be college-bound, then we could pursue community college or technical schools, which would be more economical. We figured they could work part-time or enroll in work-study to help pay for school later, and we would find another way to fund tuition, books, room, and board.

The other objection is the severity of the concept. Look at these programs from this point of view: You have a well-stocked and deluxe first aid kit as parents. You can handle—and handle well—the everyday bumps, scrapes, boo-boos, knee twists, and ankle strains. You might even be skilled enough to splint a broken finger or use a butterfly bandage or Super Glue a cut. Your first aid skills are not sufficient, however, to handle a cardiac arrest, compound fracture, or severe injuries from a fall. In the same way, parents must realize that sometimes we can't handle every discipline issue that confronts us. Your child is challenging enough. You've read everything you can to understand your child's diagnosis, you've surrounded yourself with a psychiatric and medical team, and you know your child better than anyone else. There still may come a time when you have to call 911 as a parent. These programs are the 911 for discipline issues. This is hardcore rehab for belligerent and recalcitrant children. Don't refuse to pick up the phone. Research these wilderness programs thoroughly and ask for references from other parents that have used them, then decide together the direction you should head.

Adult Children

Suddenly, your child turns eighteen. Our society considers them legal adults, yet special needs children are not typically mature at that age. You have to stay involved in their lives. There are always crises. You will have a greater role in their lives than parents of typical children. You will need to be deeply involved for their safety and continued education.

Molly is now living in a community designed for cognitively impaired adults. Recently, she got swirled up inside a situation with other residents. Gossip and rumors had turned into a text-message war. After Molly arrived home during her most recent visit, the director of the program called me. Margrey wasn't home at the time, and I was supervising Molly. The director told me that she needed to confiscate four cell phones, including Molly's. She asked me to immediately take Molly's phone from her. I was told to place it in a sealed envelope, then stow it in Molly's suitcase without her knowing. The director would retrieve Molly's cell phone from the suitcase when she returned. She planned to then go through the texts in an attempt to find the source of the gossip, rumors, and spiteful talk. After the director gave me instructions, I found Molly and asked for her phone. To Molly, her phone is life and death; asking for her phone was tantamount to me chopping off her right arm.

Even though Molly is an adult, she will sometimes revert to child-like behavior. When I asked for her phone, she screamed many obscene things, stormed off to her room, slammed the door, and reverted back to the behavior of a fourteen-year-old with very little self-control. In a matter of minutes, I heard a crash from the stairwell and found thousands of glass shards spread from the second floor to the first. I walked toward her room and heard things—perhaps books, chairs, or a suitcase—being thrown at the door.

When Molly was a teenager, one of the disciplines we employed was removing privacy as a privilege. Through the thudding and crashing behind the door, I said, "Molly, open the door, or I will remove it from its hinges." Suddenly, I was back in 2008, defusing Molly again. Sometimes this responsibility fell to me and sometimes to Margrey. I inherited the tornado this time.

She opened the door and began to spew her emotions. "I am never going back to that place. I hate it. That director is an idiot." When she was younger, something like this took two or three hours to handle.

Thankfully, this incident only took a few minutes to defuse. There is hope that the tempests your child churns will be shorter-lived as they mature. Our evening turned around once she was able to express herself. She told me her greatest fear was having her phone confiscated and not being able to talk to us every day like she does. Molly's fear is that at some point we will die, and she won't be able to talk to us in the evenings. Instead of going head to head with Molly over her phone, I came up with an alternative: she could use the facility's phone during the evenings to call us. That was solution enough for Molly at the time.

This incident is typical of life for a family with special needs or difficult children. Get used to it. Discipline will never go away. It may become less frequently needed; with consistency, it will certainly have an effect much more quickly when employed. Your desired end result is to get one child centered and the others as calm as they can be in and around the situation.

When Molly needed the most help, she destroyed many things and cut herself on the underside of her arm. I recently found an old camera Molly had, and we restored the memory card. She flipped through pictures and came across a photograph of her arms. She told me, "Dad, look at these pictures!" There

Align yourselves behind your methods of discipline.

were Xs carved shallowly into her arm from the inside of the elbow to the wrist. "Now look how my arm is. This picture is past behavior. I don't do that anymore. That's in my past. I'm much stronger now."

Moments like these with your children will remind you that what you're doing is worth all the time you have spent parenting and nurturing them. Moments like this restore your faith and allow you to see your child think more maturely. Moments like this will allow you to see progress, but this doesn't mean that your time as a parent is finished. Look at your child's progress like tread on a tire. As you drive daily, you don't notice a worn tread, but after a year or two, you can see a difference. Our hope for you is that you will look back and see drastic improvements over time in your child (and that you won't feel like a worn tire about to have a massive blowout). We call these "Molly moments," and we cherish each of them.

As teens grow into adults, we must also realize that our children's bodies are changing. They have the same mood swings as other teens. Many teens have limited coping skills. Special needs adolescents typically have even fewer coping skills and less self-awareness. Many times, we would debate whether our kids' behavior was teen-related, special needs–related, or a complex combination of both. Typically, it is the latter of the three, and it makes parenting growing children even more tenuous.

Discipline for your child is difficult. It is work for you to continually enforce and hard on your child to accept. To continue to create a strong marriage after children come along requires communication. Align yourselves behind your methods of discipline. Support each other's decisions. Share responsibility in disciplining your child. Resort to extremes when times call for it. Never undermine your spouse in the eyes of your child.

CHAPTER 14

PLAY YOUR POSITION

*The reality is you've got to play your position really well. You've
got to understand your position really well. You've got to be able to
play within a system. You have to be able to go out onto a football
field and execute a game plan within your position and for the
team and do that to a level that a coach or manager can watch
and say, "I think that I can trust that kid to play."*
—Jim McGuinness, Irish footballer

ROY

When was the last time you sat in the stands at a young kids' ballgame?
Did you see "the swarm effect"? That's where, no matter the sport, every
child on the court or field crowds around the ball. Every hand (or foot)
reaches to grab, kick, block, or shoot. You can't even see the ball because
of the swarm of kids around it. You laughingly watch the kids fight to
get the ball while the batter is freely running the bases. Coaches of this
age group spend their practices and midgame huddles reminding the little
ones to "play your position."

The refrain continues in professional athletics. A fly ball falls
between the center and right fielders because neither yells, "I've got it."

Quarterbacks are sacked because a lineman blocks the wrong opponent. Runners are disqualified because they drop the baton during the handoff.

Playing one's position is essential to success in marriage too. It closes the gap between peace and frustration. It puts more tasks in the "done" column. It creates unity rather than division.

Over the centuries, many theories and philosophies of marriage have addressed how husbands and wives should interact and how they should divide the many tasks they face in their families, churches, communities, and the world at large. That is not the purpose of this book, but this chapter can help you—today and tomorrow—to work a bit better with your mate.

Something happened during the writing of this book that is a great example of how Margrey and I have learned to play our positions. During the Christmas holidays, my mother grew very ill. She was staying with us at the time, and neither of my sisters were able to assist us with her care. On a Wednesday, I attended a doctor's appointment with my mother and heard the doctor request surgery

We spent a lot of time figuring out how our personalities and strengths worked together.

the following day. I nodded, understanding the severity of the issue, and said, "Go ahead and schedule surgery." Inside, however, I had no idea how we would now handle the events of the following day. Thursday's schedule was already spilling over, and we had just added surgery to the list:

- Molly was flying back to her home at 11:00 a.m.
- Mom's surgery was at 10:30 a.m.
- I had a scheduled surgery for a patient from 8:00 a.m. until noon.
- We had a meeting about this book at 1:00 p.m.

In addition, our niece Maria was living with us for the next semester and didn't have a car or license. She had planned to visit her cousin, who lives forty-five minutes from our house. There weren't enough hands to go around! When I got home, Margrey and I put our heads together. Margrey had already thought about some of the issues. Dylan was at home and could drive Molly to the airport. But Molly had to be accompanied to the gate, and she and Dylan could sometimes irritate each other. Maria could ride with them and walk with Molly to the gate; she is more compassionate and doesn't rub Molly the wrong way. Margrey had already pulled the necessary legal documents from our filing cabinet, written a letter to the airline, and made copies so the airport authorities would allow Maria to accompany Molly to the gate. A multitude of things could go wrong!

Dylan would wait in the lobby of the airport and then use his GPS to get Maria to her cousin's house. In the end, Dylan's help allowed Margrey to go to the hospital with my mother and me to serve my patient, who needed a significant dental surgery that could not be rescheduled. Margrey stayed at the hospital during Mom's recovery and drove her back home, while I kept the appointment for the book project and kept us moving toward our deadline. At the end of the day, we looked at what had been accomplished. Margrey and I—and our children—had *played our positions*.

What led us to work and coordinate so well during this long day? We've spent more than forty-one years stepping on each other's toes on the dance floor while we figured out each other's personalities and strengths. We spent a lot of time figuring out how our personalities and strengths *worked together*. Focusing on each other's strengths and weaknesses is not negative behavior; you are attempting to be realistic about who you are and how two independent pieces can work in precision with each other. Understanding your spouse's and your own personality types can help you in playing your position.

Personality: How We Are Wired

There are as many personality tests as colors in the rainbow. At the end of the day, taking a personality test only gives you a snapshot of your dominant style of communication and outlook on life. For the sake of our discussion, we have chosen the DiSC inventory as the thermometer we will use here.

The DiSC inventory grew out of the work of William Moulton Marston, a physiological psychologist with a PhD from Harvard. His book, *Emotions of Normal People*, published in 1928[11], laid the groundwork for the inventory to be developed. Marston hypothesized that we express our emotions through our behaviors. Those expressions could be divided into four main categories, one of which is dominant for most people. Our relationships and environment also impact how we act. The four personality types in Marston's book are listed here:

Director. Those who exhibit this behavior are direct, strong-willed, and forceful. They are extroverted and are often in charge. They are characterized as fast-paced, task-oriented, bottom-line individuals. Don't get in their way, because they can run you over.

Influencer. Influencers are sociable, talkative, and lively. They are also extroverted. They are the question askers. They are very intuitive and are the life of the party. They are spontaneous and people-oriented. They love the interactions of life. You knew them in high school and called them cheerleaders. Influencers are generally touchy-feely people.

Steadiness. Individuals in this area are amiable. They are the peacemakers and are not comfortable making waves. They are gentle, accommodating, and soft-hearted. They are often more introverted and are rarely confrontational. They are more slow-paced and are people-oriented.

Conscientiousness. These conscientious or cautious people tend to be more introverted as well. They are analytical. They often plod through decisions and fear making a wrong decision due to a lack of information. They love data and studying it. They are slower-paced and task-oriented. These individuals may often pursue an accounting or science career.

---

[11] Marston, William Moulton, London, K. Paul, Trench, Trubner & Co.; New York, Harcourt, Brace and Co., 1928.

One personality type is not better than another. In a family, classroom, or office, you often need a mix of all four personality types to operate smoothly. Conflict arises when different personalities battle each other or rub each other the wrong way. This is a natural consequence of communicating differently.

Each of us is a mixture of all four personalities, and we generally have a primary and secondary style. There are no better or worse classifications or personalities, and the general population falls about 25 percent into any one category. Margrey's dominant style is Director, and her secondary style is Influencer. Margrey doesn't ask questions; she gives directions and opinions:

"Tomorrow is garbage day. Take out the garbage."

"Roy, take that mail with you to the office tomorrow. It needs to go out fast."

This happens so often I don't even hear it. Margrey makes decisions quickly and moves forward. On the other hand, I am primarily Conscientious and secondarily a Director. I'm much more of a plodder; I work cautiously and analyze a situation much more than Margrey. I tend to ask questions and avoid direct confrontation:

"Margrey, can you grab me some water from the kitchen?"

"Margrey, what time do you feel we should leave tomorrow?"

Our favorite argument is, "Who's going to be in charge today?" Our standard comment upon giving up authority to the other is, "Great, I'll do it your way *again*!" Margrey's mind is like a steel trap when it comes to her schedule, event details, and the nuances of people's lives. I know the computer well and can pretty much find anything on it. I send out the Christmas letter and cards and keep up with addresses. I was too busy during a recent Christmas season to do it, and so we didn't send cards. Margrey neither considered nor had the desire to take on this detailed task.

When the children misbehaved in their youth, Margrey's justice was fast and unwavering, whereas I tended to discuss their behaviors more in an effort to teach them better. We jokingly laugh that the children would look at Margrey and say, "Go ahead and punish me before Dad gets home, so he won't talk to me for thirty minutes."

Knowing these differences allows us to appreciate the each other's strengths and to laugh at our weaknesses. How many times has Margrey reminded me of something that I forget ten minutes later? How many times have I showed her how to scan a document with her phone and email it? Neither of us has *all* the answers. God created marriage and gave you a mate for a reason. Rearrange the letters from the word *mate*, and you get the word *team*. On a team, everyone has a position to play. The coach doesn't move the catcher to pitcher position unless he wants to experience failure. Don't divide tasks in your marriage in a way that leads to failure! Talk to your spouse, listen to each other, and then use your strengths and work to improve your weaknesses.

Remember, no two human beings are exactly alike, and this inventory is only one measurement of a person. Don't allow the DiSC theory to put you into a box or stick a label on you! Use it to understand and appreciate yourself and your spouse and each other's behaviors more deeply.

There are dozens of free versions of the DiSC inventory on the internet. Just for fun, before reading more of this chapter, sit down tonight with your spouse and take one of the free tests to discover what your types are. Then read the rest of the chapter to learn how to work better together.

Strengths and Weaknesses

An important part of playing your position is knowing what position you have the *ability* to play. Everyone has strengths and weaknesses. I am into minute details; Margrey sees a bigger picture. In writing this book, Margrey liked telling a story and having someone else write it down. For my part, I'm more of a control freak.

Strengths should be celebrated. If a person is an amazing chef but isn't any good at soccer, that person is applauded for his or her culinary ability; the lack of athletic skills is not an issue. However, when it comes to personality traits, we too often expect everyone to have all of them. Don't ask the introvert to take on tasks that call for an extrovert. If your spouse is strong in one area, don't expect them to be strong in all areas. Celebrate the differences between you. Realize that your children will develop a primary personality type also. Knowing their personality types will help you communicate with them more effectively. In the same manner, where you are weak does not mean you are deficient in any way. You are wired for your strengths.

How the Styles Work Together

For the sake of our discussion here on playing your position, let's look at how one major factor in your personality style—introversion versus extroversion—blends with your spouse's and the difficulties and joys that come from the mixture.

When Both of You Are Extroverts. On the outside, you might be seen as a power couple. You're out and about; you know lots of people and make lots of connections. Life is fast-paced and fun. You recharge around other people or in the middle of activity.

What is good? Your skill with relationships means that you are getting to know the best doctors and practitioners for your children. You are hearing about new techniques, programs, camps, and medicines that others might not hear about. You feel connected to a community and have support around you.

What might be lacking? Your pace may be so fast you could run through a danger sign without even seeing the words. When two extroverts get together, they are often less analytical than if each was working alone. You may be paced much faster than your children, and your ability to multitask may frustrate them if they transition much more slowly than you.

How do you see the holes? You've got to breathe. Remember the big picture, your right-sized goals, and your most important desires. Pull back and look at what you've learned. Have you implemented too many changes simply for the sake of change? Cheer each other on and encourage each other. Be intentional about rest and about listening to each other and your children.

When Both of You Are Introverts. Although a misconception, from the outside your quieter and more somber temperament may be seen as lack of leadership, or people might think you're weak. In many situations, one of you will need to take the lead. You recharge in private, away from other people.

What is good? You are careful and precise. Your child has never missed a dose of medicine and, as far as it depends on you, has never been late to a practitioner's appointment (or even school, for that matter).

What might be lacking? When two introverts blend, sometimes words go unspoken with one another. You may hold back and not say something for the risk of offending the other or out of fear of the ramifications. Two introverts can also isolate from the world. Circling the wagons is good against an attack, but you need a support system around you.

How do you see the holes? You must step out of your comfort zone and talk with others. Ask more questions of your doctors, attend more support group meetings or seminars, and talk about your struggles with those you trust. Be willing to try something new two or more times a year for the sake of your relationship and your children's overall health.

When One of You Is an Introvert and the Other Is an Extrovert. Although opposites are said to attract, different personalities can clash at times. Respect each other's special gifts and what they can bring to your relationship.

What is good? You cause each other to stretch. The extrovert drags the introvert out for more connection. The introvert has more information to analyze, which helps both of you make better decisions.

What might be lacking? There are more sparks per cubic inch in this type of relationship than any other. Sometimes peace is hard to achieve unless you realize your differences and play to your strengths. The extrovert wants to drive ahead; the introvert wants to analyze more or has trouble convincing the extrovert of new facts and data.

How do you see the holes? Give the introvert time to recharge in private between large-group or high-octane settings. Set aside time to talk in private. If the extrovert can listen deeply and patiently, the introvert will feel heard. As an introvert realize that your partner may move faster and more boldly than you. At times this boldness can be an advantage in your relationship and your parenting.

Compromise, Don't Criticize

When my mother visits our house, Margrey and I give her free rein to wash clothes, fold them in any particular way, and put them away. She can load the dishwasher in the order she chooses. We are not overly concerned about having a certain color of towel in a certain bathroom. We are glad to have Mom at the house, so we take what we get when she helps.

Likewise, if Margrey is cooking, I'm not going to complain about the food. If I clean the garage or the yard, she does not "snoopervise" me. Trust counts in relationships. Trust and compromise allow partners to play to their strengths. Knowing your spouse's personality can help you not only understand and accept their strengths but also celebrate the differences they bring into the relationship.

Understanding Your Child

Once you get a grip on your own personality style and how it blends with your spouse's style, there's another helpful step. Learn your *child's* personality, and study the ways you blend well with them—and the ways you cause confusion and pain in the relationship due to misunderstandings. You can reduce a lot of frustration and learn how to deliver information better through this process.

When your child is in their midteens, it may be interesting and helpful for them to take the inventory (there are age-specific inventories available), but many parents have a better experience reading up on the different styles and coming to a conclusion without an inventory. When your child reaches the teen years, an inventory can be a helpful tool for your child's understanding of themselves, as well.

As Heather, Dylan and Molly have matured it is interesting watching how they assimilate and process information and deal with stress or confrontation. While one may run from conflict another hits it head on. Our style of communicating differently with each and staying aware of their personality traits helps keep our relationships with them intact and healthy.

Stay Friends Forever

When you got married, every thought was about being together. The photographs showed you arm in arm, leaning into each other or laughing. The thought probably never crossed your mind that one day your spouse could become your adversary, but a few years into marriage with a child in the house, many couples begin to feel they are working *against* each other instead of *with* each other. All the personality traits we noticed when we were dating and thought were cute can later begin to grind on our nerves a bit. We can easily begin to look at our spouse's strengths as weaknesses, not as ways their skills can build our parenting and marriage team.

"Your mate is not your enemy."

Author, speaker, and radio host Dennis Rainey is fond of reminding couples, "Your mate is not your enemy." Too often, enemy status is assigned because of personality differences. Your spouse makes decisions differently than you do or does things in a different order and at a different pace than you do. Maybe their first thought is about the task and yours is about the people.

Don't look at your mate as your enemy. See them correctly, full of strengths and love for you. Find ways to work together to solve the problems that you face in your marriage and your parenting. At the end of the day, if you did everything the way your spouse wanted to do it to get the job done and it was successful, who cares? Let go of having to have everything done your way. Let go of control. If you play your position—and let your spouse play the one created for them—you'll have more peace, get more accomplished, and have a more fulfilling and lasting marriage.

CHAPTER 15

MANAGE TIME WITH FEROCITY

You get to decide where your time goes.
You can either spend it moving forward,
or you can spend it putting out fires.
You decide. And if you don't decide,
others will decide for you.
—Tony Morgan, *pastor and church consultant*

ROY

There are as many books on time and task management as there are words in this book. "There is no new thing under the sun!"[12] In the way that weight loss can be summed up as "eat better, eat less, and exercise more," so time and task management can be summed up as "write every task down, say no often, focus, and work hard." However, time management for the parent of a child with learning, developmental, or psychological challenges is as important as breathing. If you don't own and direct your calendar, you won't be able to breathe. Cooperative time management

---

[12] Ecclesiastes 1:9 (KJV).

between you and your spouse must become a daily routine, like tying your shoes or brushing your teeth.

As employers, we both wish that every employee managed time better. We wish we managed our own tasks and calendars better. The concepts we address here are things each of us can do better every day.

We have already discussed personality types and how they affect communication and conflict within the marriage relationship and in your ability to get through to your child. In a similar fashion, you and your spouse may have different time management methods. Margrey has an uncanny ability to hear something and log it in her memory. She can recall many levels of detail. I don't; if there is more than one layer to a task, I need it written down. My constant refrain to Margrey is, "Did you write it on my list?"

For example, Margrey came to me recently and said, "Here are the three letters we talked about mailing this weekend. The first one doesn't have the address. I don't have it anywhere. You'll need to call Julie to get the address. It should go in the regular mail; the second one needs to go overnight; and the third one has that book, and it can go the cheapest way possible."

I was lost somewhere in the first sentence, trying to remember who Julie was. I said, "Margrey, hold on a second, I need this written down."

Even after forty-one years together, she said, "It's easy, all you need to remember is . . ." That woman amazes me! She's able to hold and process intricate details in her mind or on paper but not in the computer. I'd rather have a complicated computer schedule and a detailed to-do list.

How about you and your spouse? How do you manage time and tasks differently? Who is the spontaneous one? Who is the forgetful one? Does one of you underestimate or overestimate the amount of time a task requires? How do both of you feel about deadlines or about being early for appointments? These and hundreds of other questions reveal how each of you looks at time. Set a date on your schedule now to sit down and look at just one week in your recent past. What was on the calendar? How did you handle it? Did you accomplish what you had planned? Where did you succeed or fall short? Where is improvement needed? Gain an understanding of what happened and why it happened the way it did to inform you as you move forward.

So many of us work on things that are less than important. Sometimes, knocking these lesser things off the to-do list helps you gain traction so that you can dig into the important tasks with momentum. Other times, by doing so, you may be keeping yourself off balance. Raising a special needs child takes focus and attention on the critical issues.

Differences between how you and your spouse view time will also reveal themselves in how you track things. Just walk into an office products store, and you'll see the variety of ways to keep track of your life: journals, Post-It notes, page-a-day calendars, wall calendars, smartphones, and more.

About two years ago, I fully converted to an electronic calendar so that I can update events from anywhere. If it's not in my phone, it's like I don't know about it. I recently traveled to New Orleans for a meeting. I showed up at the first event wearing a suit and tie. Everyone else was dressed casually. I joked with my cohorts that the dress code didn't make it into my schedule.

Margrey, on the other hand, has everything written down in a very small pocket calendar book. I can't follow her logic or her schedule. It looks like she has items written on top of each other. Nevertheless, she never misses an appointment and always knows everything that's going on.

Don't let either of these issues cause friction in your relationship. Embrace technological differences in the same way you embrace the differences between the ways you remember and your personality styles. No matter how you handle time and task management in the trenches, this chapter outlines the areas where you need to be thinking and executing.

Goal Setting

Setting annual goals is only important for those who want to succeed in life. That's a big statement that might cause you to bristle if you've never set out a twelve-month plan. As important as this is, the way you tackle it will be as different as the two of you are. I take time, write everything down, and come up with a guiding document for the year with a tracking methodology attached. Margrey does no such thing, but if you talked with her about these issues, you would hear crystal-clear objectives.

Around October of every year, I begin thinking about the coming year. I make notes about the things I want to accomplish. I break ideas into seven categories:

- Spiritual Life
- Marriage
- Children
- Business
- Mind
- Body
- Finances

When I start the process, I may have dozens of ideas. I think and pray about the ideas until I narrow them down. I might end the process with four goals in one area but only one goal under another heading. Some years, I might not have a single goal in one category, because another goal crosses over into that territory. Before I implement any of the goals, I then look at the entire year. I think about Margrey's needs and about my children's needs. I seriously attempt to look at my weaknesses, and I set goals to address these. For example, one recent year was going to be largely absorbed by the expansion of my dental practice. This would take much, but not all, of my focus. I trimmed my goals to suit the larger objective for the year.

As part of my goals, I pick a single word to focus on yearly. My attempt is for it to intentionally permeate other goals in my life throughout the

Setting annual goals is only important for those who want to succeed in life.

year. Past words have included Simplify, Humility, and Focus. Be bold, and set goals outside of your comfort zone!

Potential Pitfalls of Goal Setting

Goal setting alone doesn't ensure success. I feel reviewing your goals regularly is imperative to success. Place them where you will see them weekly or more often. Redefining your goals as you move through the year can keep you on target. Taking a goal off the list isn't failure; it's a recalibration of what's possible. Sometimes you will find you were much too conservative and sometimes you will see you were much too agressive in your goals. Through the years I've spotted five pitfalls of time and task management and goal setting.

1. **Not sharing your plan with your spouse.** The scary part of my goal-setting comes when I share my goals with Margrey. She's never critical, but she's the only one that sees all my goals. They are both personal and private. Some goals are shared with my office team or close friends, but most are just for me.

   "If you fail to plan, you plan to fail."

   Sharing goals invites accountability and opens you up to questions. Some think, "If I don't share my goals, then if I fail to hit them, it won't matter as much." Don't set goals to not hit them! You've set goals for a reason: you want to grow and get things done. There is a saying that rings true: "If you fail to plan, you plan to fail." Share your goals with your spouse, and talk about them when you talk about your calendar and finances.

2. **Not listening to the wisdom of your spouse.** Your husband or wife knows you better than anyone else on the planet. They see your strengths and weaknesses with great clarity. Inside your safe marriage, listen to your spouse's opinion about what you have

planned and what you're capable of. Take those observations above all others as you finalize your plan. Hopefully you will have a spouse that will push you and support you in whatever goals you've set. This is part of the trust equation. You must trust your spouse to encourage and support you and to never undermine your aspirations. Equally important is the fact that your spouse can keep you realistic by lovingly reminding you of your weaknesses. I never leave enough time for errands; I get distracted and put something on my list that wasn't there when I left home. I see a friend and spend too much time talking to them. All my tasks take me longer than I estimate. Listen to your subconscious and follow your gut in the same way you listen to your spouse.

3. **Having too many things on your list.** Focus is essential. God has designed our minds to process information on multiple levels. Air traffic controllers are aware of their assigned flights, the weather, schedule delays on the ground, and more. Elementary school teachers manage the needs and learning styles of all their students simultaneously. However, in both examples, one shouldn't overload these highly trained individuals. An air traffic controller can't manage one hundred flights at once, and an elementary school teacher can't thrive with sixty students in a class. In the same way, you can have too many goals. Even when you have goals in many different areas of life, you must find an ebb and flow in which goals you focus on at which time. Success comes, though, when you do focus on the most important things in your life. Listen to your spouse and other trusted individuals to make sure your focus won't be spread too thin. I've also learned that by the end of the year, you will have accomplished other items that never even made it onto your radar during the planning process. Life is full of curves! A wise goal-setter leaves margin for these items.

4. **Setting your goals too high.** Be wary of goals set too high. But wait—you can't set goals too high! I love gigantic, enormous, obscene goals. But you can set *unreasonable* goals. You can set an unreasonable timetable to *accomplish* your goals. For example,

if you want to grow your emergency financial fund, you may set a goal to have six months' living expenses in the bank by the end of the year. That would mean that fifty percent of your income goes into savings. For most of us, this is way too aggressive and thus too high of a goal. Yet even in this case, if you and your wife both take second jobs and cut expenses, you could be well on your way to meeting this goal. Ensure that your goals are realistic for where you are and the time you have to accomplish them. In a special needs family, you should not throw caution to the wind. Always plan cautiously for the unexpected.

In addition, you may set big goals for yourself, but be reasonable in what you feel your children can accomplish. Our goals for our children are much more general, but the idea is to get them thinking about goals. Their goals may be about following directions better, using better table manners, spending their allowance more wisely, or flushing the toilet. Also be realistic in knowing that your children will absorb much of your time.

5. **Feeling discouraged.** Zig Ziglar often said, "He who aims at nothing hits it every time." You will not hit all of your goals; that's just fine. You made progress. You did something! Recently one year, I set a goal to read one book per week; I read forty-two books. I could be discouraged that I fell short by ten books, or I could marvel that I have read forty-two books that have helped me grow in knowledge.

I review my goals regularly throughout the year, and at the end of the year, I evaluate my progress. I do this both to celebrate my accomplishments and to investigate and study what was missed, as well as to plan for the upcoming year. Occasionally, I have totally abandoned a goal during the year, but at the end of the year, I mark every goal with one of three words: *Good*, *Great*, or *Terrible*.

I then write a sentence about each goal that I marked as *Terrible*. I think about why it was not accomplished or not accomplished well. Should I have tried harder? Did I forget that I set the goal? Did that task play to one of my weaknesses? Did I just have no passion about the goal? Honest self-assessment is critical to being stronger the following year.

Annual Calendar Planning

Chances are you and/or your spouse have a career outside of the home. Each year, you have at your discretion only so many vacation days, sick days, personal days, or paid time off (PTO) days, depending on what your employer calls them. Whether or not you know it, many of your free days are already claimed by vacation, doctor visits, your holiday traditions, school field trips, out-of-town activities, summer camps, and more.

You and your spouse need to get ahead of the game and not let these items surprise you. I've heard stories of those who didn't put their time-off requests in soon enough and lost out on great opportunities. I've listened to friends brainstorm about how to get more time off, because all of their days are used and there's more life to be lived in the year. Yes, there are many things coming up in the next twelve months you don't have dates for, but you've got to get ahead of the curve. The reality is, if you sat down and marked everything out on the schedule as you needed it, you would exceed your discretionary days.

You know life is complicated enough, so you must plan ahead. We've talked about pregaming how to get your family out the door for church or a recital. Managing the annual calendar is pregaming at its very best: pregaming your *year*. Pregaming your year will allow you to find rest as well. It will allow you to locate private and quiet time—*necessary* time—for you and your spouse.

Getting Things Done

By being thoughtful, committing goals to paper, having goals in several categories, reviewing them regularly and adjusting them appropriately through the year you will set your self up for success. Following are some other thoughts that will put you and your family on the path to success.

Nightly Debrief. One constant refrain in this book is the nightly debrief. We've brought this up before, but we're amazed at how much we mess up and how much miscommunication occurs when we miss it. We're also amazed at how many couples don't do it and just let life happen.

We start getting ready for bed about 8:00 p.m. but are awake till at least 9:30 p.m. We're not watching television, but it might be on for background noise. During this time, we talk about what did or didn't happen during the day. What was missed? How could we have done better? This is a problem-solving time and a time for celebrating the victories of the day. It's a time to give thanks for our health and our lives. We rarely allow this time to become negative. We discuss the calendar during this time too—what's happening the next day or next week and what is the next big event coming our way. Begin planning who will drive which child to what event, think about taking one or two cars to an event, and consider any small logistical problems that may arise in the coming days and undermine your success. As we wind down the day, we may be reading, texting, or planning tomorrow mentally, but we easily spend an hour or two in the bedroom just aligning our minds. We are not strictly business, though! Some nights we break out of our ritual and are spontaneous.

Sometimes even the regular events need to be brought up. Am I going to Rotary Club on Tuesday morning or not? Is Margrey attending her Bible study or book club this week? Is this the week I have study club? Recently, Margrey reminded me that we were committed to attend a wedding the following weekend.

"Did you put it on the calendar?" I asked.

"No, but I've told you four times."

"If you had put it on the computer, it would be on my phone and I would know about it."

"But I don't use your electronic calendar."

It was an old and oft-repeated conflict. I just grabbed my phone and entered the wedding into my calendar. As married couples, we can't let these matters send us into a cycle of disconnection or debate. There's not enough time for that. Our time has to be reserved for and focused on the children. They are much more important than arguing about a lapse in our scheduling.

Sunday night reviews of the calendar and to-do list are the most important. We are preparing for the work and school week. Are you ready for the next week? I have restless nights on Sundays when I am not fully prepared for the week.

Put a Target Date on Everything. For example, the webbing on your son's catcher's mitt comes loose at practice on Tuesday night, and he has a game on Saturday. The catcher's mitt must be repaired. When will you do it? Once you realize you have a task, stop, look at your calendar, and plan on it. Then bring it up at your next nightly debrief.

You may have to go through this process twenty times a week in order to capture everything life throws at you! Have your calendar handy as you're going through your child's school planner and when you look over the bulletin on Sunday morning at church.

Consider the "Eisenhower Box." Many time- and task-management authors point to the four-celled "Eisenhower Box" as an essential decision-making tool. During Dwight D. Eisenhower's tenure as the Allied Forces supreme commander during World War II, he was faced with critical decision after critical decision. He developed this matrix to help him sort through the issues that needed his attention. When you are faced with a new task or an annual goal, it falls into one of four categories:

Quadrant I: Both urgent and important
Quadrant II: Not urgent but still important
Quadrant III: Urgent but not important
Quadrant IV: Neither urgent nor important

Focus most of your time on Quadrant I, tasks that are both urgent and important. These are your *top* priorities. Quadrant II, items that are not urgent but still important, should be scheduled next; find the time soon

THE EISENHOWER BOX

	URGENT	NOT URGENT
IMPORTANT	**DO** *Do it now.* Write article for today.	**DECIDE** *Schedule a time to do it.* Exercising. Calling family and friends. Researching articles. Long-term biz strategy.
NOT IMPORTANT	**DELEGATE** *Who can do it for you?* Scheduling interviews. Booking flights. Approving comments. Answering certain emails. Sharing articles.	**DELETE** *Eliminate it.* Watching television. Checking social media. Sorting through junk mail.

to do these tasks before they rise to Quadrant I. For tasks that are urgent but not important (Quadrant III), see if there is someone else that can do this for you. Don't think you must do everything for everyone! If you have the luxury of delegating, do so. If there's something on your list in Quadrant IV—the items that are neither important nor urgent—don't do them. Get these items off your list. Do your best to remain in Quadrants I and II. These are the most critical areas, where you can be most effective and influential in your life.

Curveballs. There are few things so critical in our schedule that we can't cancel them. No person or thing is that important. Life happens. Author C. S. Lewis once wrote, "The great thing, if one can, is to stop regarding all the unpleasant things as interruptions of one's 'own' or 'real' life. The truth is of course that what one calls the interruptions are precisely one's real life—the life God is sending day by day."[13]

---

[13] Lewis, C.S., Letters of C. S. Lewis, Harcourt Publishing, 1966.

Being flexible doesn't mean you throw a task or goal away just for the heck of it. Remember that your relationship with your spouse and your relationship with your children are more important than the tasks at hand. Keep the relationship primary and your schedule flexible. When a task gets delayed, don't just let it go; open your calendar and assign a new date for it. I also recommend writing down *why* you moved it. When it comes up again, this explanation will give you strength and power to better accomplish it.

Keeping Your Child on Schedule. With children like ours, we went through a lot of drama and trauma. One morning, as we were getting ready for school, Dylan refused to get dressed because he didn't like the pants he was supposed to put on. Time ticked by until it was time to go, so Margrey said, "Okay, then, you can go to school in your underwear." She loaded everyone up and drove the two blocks to the bus stop. Dylan didn't know that Margrey had his clothes with her. Molly and Heather kept asking him if he was really going to school in his underwear. As the time drew near for the bus to arrive, Dylan fumed, refusing to get out of the car with even more energy than he'd used refusing to put on his pants at the house. He sweated long enough, and then Margrey handed him his pants. He was much less picky about his clothes after that.

One Saturday, I walked through the kitchen and saw the trash can overflowing. That was one of Dylan's chores. I reminded him that he needed to take the trash out. He yelled from upstairs, "I'll do it in a little while." I ran my errands and came back about two hours later, and the trash was still there. Procrastination is such an enemy! Tempted as I was to empty the trash myself and be done with the chore, I called Dylan down and watched as he took the trash out.

Here are some techniques for keeping your child on task:

- Don't forget pregaming.
- Start much earlier than you think you need to.

- Think through everything that can go wrong, and prepare contingencies for each.
- Communicate several times what needs to happen.
- Have your child repeat directions back to you so you know they heard and understood.

Roadblocks to Getting It Done

Distraction. Right now, I have three letters I need to write to other doctors. I am trying to find every reason possible to not write these letters. The first two will take at least thirty minutes each. The third will require about two hours of research. This is at least three hours of work! I could do so many other things that I would enjoy far more. However, I promised my team that those letters would be ready to mail on Monday, so I have to suck it up and do it. If I do, I will feel a sense of accomplishment. Endorphins will be released after I complete the task, and I will have more energy throughout the day to do the things I want to do. *Just do it!*

You will always have distractions. In the moment, a distraction may feel like an essential. The Eisenhower Box can come in handy to evaluate potential distractions. Is it in Quadrant I or II? Then press on. Is it neither urgent nor important? If so, put it away.

Don't fall into the trap of labeling rest as a distraction. It's good and necessary to take a nap from time to time. Relax a little; make time to read a book; take a walk. Those tasks are important, but they are not urgent. They make life bearable and recharge your batteries for the harder tasks.

Knowing How Much Time You Need. Margrey has an uncanny ability to measure the potential time it will take to complete a task. I frequently underestimate how long a task will take. Which do you do?

If you're like me, add 20-percent more time to the task when you put it on your calendar than you think you need. Discuss the time allotment with your spouse during your nightly debrief as well. Just think, the worst thing that could happen would be you finish early and have time for rest or another task.

Not Letting Things Go. There are some photographs on the servers at my office, more on CDs in a box, and even more on the backup hard drive at the house. I have the task of organizing all these photos on my to-do list. It's been on my to-do list for about ten years. I would love to sit down and take the hours to get it done. I wouldn't be surprised if it is still on my to-do list when I retire. Sometimes I worry that the server will melt down or the hard drive at home will crash, but nonetheless, compared to the rest of our calendar, sorting those pictures just isn't that important or urgent—and I do have multiple backups.

Let yourself off the hook for the items on your to-do list like these pictures. Strike them off or move them to a list of things to do someday in the future. Life is too short to carry the burden of a handful—or even a truckload—of tasks you can let go.

Perfectionism. You will never be perfect. You will never complete your tasks to perfection. I've seen that perfectionism comes often from a selfish motivation; someone who strives for perfection finds their value in the completed task. If it's not perfect, they have less worth. Having a high standard of excellence, on the other hand, is about the task. Have a high standard! I do—as a dentist, I strive for 100-percent success on every dental procedure. Over the course of my career, however, I've had to accept that a self-evaluated score of 95 percent has to be enough. I have to count it as a roaring success! Baseball players that can hit the ball 33 percent of the time are considered exceptional hitters. Why, then, should my 95 percent not be considered a success?

Perfectionists often don't finish tasks either. They think, "If I can't do it perfectly, I shouldn't do it at all." A completed task has infinitely more value than an uncompleted one, no matter how perfect the incomplete one might have been.

Getting Help. Throughout this book, we've talked about the importance of your team. Time management is also a team sport, and there will be times where you need more help in order to accomplish everything that's going on. Your team might include the following:

- Older siblings
- Nannies or babysitters
- Extended family (parents, in-laws, aunts, and uncles)
- Friends or neighbors
- Employees or coworkers
- Church community
- Professionals

Your children know who their parents are. Sometimes you can't be there in person, but you're present with your encouragement, prayers, and focused attention and questions afterward.

I am just as capable of braiding my daughter's hair as Margrey is. I'm not as talented at it as Margrey, but the hair is acceptable. Margrey is just as capable of taking Dylan to a baseball game and screaming from the stands as I am. Her cheering means just as much as if not more than mine.

One day, Heather called me at the office. "Dad, I need you to bring me some clean underwear and jeans—and can you hurry?"

What had happened? "Why now?" I asked.

"Well, I'm . . ."

I inhaled deeply and thought, *You've become a woman, and you called me.* I then said, "Where is your mom?"

"She's at that meeting, remember?"

"Right. I'll take care of it." As I hung up the phone, I thanked God that our children are comfortable with either one of us helping them with any issue. I enlisted the help of one of my employees and sent her to the house, where she gathered the necessary clothes and supplies and carried them to the school while I completed patient care. Utilize the tools at your disposal and enlist the people necessary to get the job done.

The clock starts over every morning when your alarm goes off. You will make mistakes in time management. Some days will test your endurance.

There will be days when you don't accomplish anything on your task list because your child melted down and you spent hours in the return to status quo. Don't let it shake you! Just start over the next day.

There were so many days when Margrey would be so tired as she got ready for bed. The day had gotten the best of her, and she was exhausted and out of ideas. She would say, "Roy, I just don't know how I'm going to get through tomorrow." And yet, the celebration of Lamentations 3:22–23 awaits: his mercies "are new every morning." She always awoke with at least one new idea.

Accomplish what you can. The Benedictine monks describe their lives as *ora et labora*—pray and work. Work like it all depends on you; pray because it all depends on Him.

CHAPTER 16

LEARN CONSTANTLY

All I have learned, I learned from books.
—Abraham Lincoln

ROY

"I don't know"—as a dentist and perfectionist, I don't like to say this! Whether you say it out loud or feel it in your gut, parents like us are intimately familiar with these words. Every doctor's appointment, counseling session, and phone call from a teacher brings the phrase back to the forefront. Every time a new behavior management plan doesn't work or a medicine produces a side effect, these words echo inside.

Years ago, I was taught a simple phrase, and the concept behind the phrase transformed the words from dark to hopeful: "I don't know, but I'll find out."

When it comes to staying married and rearing children, we must always be learning—*always*. We will never learn the contents of a single library or see the end of the internet, but God made our brains big enough to absorb new facts, figures, ideas, and stories our entire lives. This lifelong learning is like carrying a tool box with you at all times. You'll have more tools and resources available when situations, crises, and celebrations come your way.

Why Is Lifelong Learning Important?

Our world is changing at a dizzying rate. No, marriage and parenting aren't like nanotechnology or robotic brain surgery, but discoveries abound. New medications, new ways of communicating, new laws, and new opportunities are plentiful. Most likely, there is also much previously existing information we haven't yet learned. Many tried and tested techniques contain wisdom that we can tap into.

In whatever employment situation you may find yourself, constant learning and improvement is imperative. Would you have the bravado to tell your employer, "This is the best I'll ever be. I'll never accomplish anything more efficiently or better than I do today. And by the way, I do expect a salary increase year after year"? (Please don't attempt this, as it could lead to unemployment quickly!) As a dentist or an individual, I will never come to believe that I need to quit learning. If I ever speak to a patient and suggest that today is the best I'll ever be, my suggestion is that they fire me and find another dentist that thirsts for knowledge. As I mentioned in an earlier chapter, Margrey's father always said that when you stop learning and moving, you should start building a pine box. This same attitude should permeate your marriage and your parenting. Always look for learning opportunities.

Becoming a lifelong learner is not only about becoming better at academics but also about application to life. Becoming a lifelong learner isn't about writing essays and solving equations; it's about finding the missing pieces to your life's puzzle. Always be thirsty for knowledge. Be on the lookout for learning opportunities. With children we call these teachable moments and it's our obligation to teach them yet as adults we must be responsible for teaching ourselves. Learning is about introspective analysis of your weaknesses and strengths. Learning is about changing and adapting over time yet not for the sake of change but as a quest for improvement.

Constant learning as an adult takes time, but it doesn't always require time in large chunks. You already have enough time taken away from your life. Learning requires commitment and diligence, but it can fit into life's cracks.

How Do I Learn Now?

You are already a lifelong learner, even if you don't consider yourself one. You are taking in new information, processing it, and applying it to your life. If you've tried one of the delicious recipes that show up on your Facebook feed, you're learning. If you've had a conversation with a friend about a new medication, you're learning. If you are visiting with a friend and you remember something interesting about him or her, you are learning. We encourage you to make it purposeful and not accidental. Flip a switch in your mind and begin to learn on purpose. Here are some methods to experiment with.

Books. Books will provide you with unending knowledge. There are books on every subject imaginable. Many Americans read as few as one book each year! The books need not be of epic length. Many beneficial books are less than two hundred pages long. If you read just ten pages a day, you can easily read a book a month. Your reading doesn't need to be about learning, necessarily; some reading can be done strictly for escape and pleasure. You can travel to distant places and experience different facets of life through reading about someone else's adventures. If you have a friend that has never learned to read, this could present you an opportunity to enroll them in a literacy program so that they too can learn from books. Continual learning and self-improvement will also make you a more interesting and desirable spouse.

Audiobooks. Audiobooks have long been a secret weapon for those who are too busy to learn through reading. Lack of technology, though, kept many audiobooks from being produced and made them expensive to purchase. Those who loved audiobooks struggled to keep up with all of the cassettes and CDs they required. The internet has revolutionized the industry; audiobooks are now inexpensive to create and distribute.

Smartphones have made them portable and weightless. Audiobooks are now the fastest-growing segment in publishing.

For years, educators called audiobooks cheating or criticized them for not being as rigorous for students as processing the written word, but research into learning styles and dyslexia has proven that an audiobook listener must accomplish all the most important tasks that a paper book reader does: taking in information, understanding concepts, and critically thinking about the material. No, you can't underline or highlight an audiobook while you listen, but most audiobook apps allow you to create bookmarks. Some allow you to add typed notes!

Notetaking and Journaling. Much of your learning related to your child will take place face to face with doctors, counselors, and experts. Information flows from their brains and mouths faster than the legal disclaimers at the end of radio commercials. Capturing their words will accelerate your understanding and help him improve your care of your child. Carry a small notebook and pen with you wherever you go; after your conversation with someone, jot down the most important things you remember. Don't be embarrassed to take notes while they are talking to you. Consider using your smartphone's voice recorder app to record the practitioner's words so you can listen again and take even *more* detailed notes. Put a date on every page so you can rebuild the timeline of treatment when needed.

As we've said numerous times, you know your child best. You are with them more hours than anyone else. You pick up on their facial expressions and sighs. When they are ill, you know what temperature on the thermometer means they have a fever, even if the internet doesn't agree. However, sometimes you can't put your finger on a problem, issue, or side effect without recording your observations. Get into the habit of jotting down a few words every day—journaling—about your child's condition or mood. Those notes may prove to be priceless the next time you visit with one of the professionals on your team. Many physicians may ask that you record time and behavior in a journal to assist them in tweaking medication dosages and intervals. Use your journal for jotting down questions for your doctors as well. Highlight these questions so they come to mind quickly at your child's next doctor visit.

Conferences and Seminars. We believe in conferences and seminars. The dedicated time away from the pressures of work and family focuses your attention on learning. A good conference experience compresses the value of several books into just a few hours. The concentrated dose of content will go deeper into your memory and will be applied more effectively. Do the following things to make the most of a seminar:

- Attend every main session and take a few notes in each one. Jot down your questions in the margins of handouts or on your notepad.
- If there are breakout sessions, you and your spouse should "divide and conquer" so you can go to more sessions and share notes over dinner.
- Talk with others who attend. Invite them to share their stories, and don't be afraid to share yours. If you connect with someone, exchange contact information, because having more allies is always a good thing. As you build trust with your fellow conference guests, consider discussing your questions.
- If you get a few minutes with the presenter, ask your most pressing question.
- Don't forget to rest. A conference is a chance not only to learn but to relax. Don't fill all the free time at a conference with work; breathe, nap, and talk.
- Purchase the audio and/or video recordings of the seminar, and schedule a time in the following thirty days to review one or two of the sessions with your spouse.
- Ask your child's physician or teacher about upcoming conferences that would be beneficial to your child's situation. Check with your local university, hospital, or support group for potential programs.

Podcasts and Webinars. Many short learning opportunities are available in this format, and many are less than an hour. These can be downloaded to a mobile device and watched or listened to anywhere. You can listen to podcasts while driving your kids to school or waiting in line for school to get out. If there is a wait in your physician's or dentist's office, you may be able to get in a few minutes of learning time. When we look with an open mind, we will find that the world of learning is limitless.

Online Reading: The Good, the Bad, and the Distracting. Since the advent of the newspaper, pundits have said, "Don't believe everything you read." That's certainly true about what we read on the internet! The web is a great source for information and answers to questions, but it can also be like walking into an old barn filled with spiderwebs—or worse yet, stepping into cow manure.

As you search online, read (or watch) with your eyes open and consider these red flags:

- **Sensational headlines.** "The parents were on top of their child when the police arrived. You'll be SHOCKED at what happened next." These provocative headlines get more clicks than regular ones, but beware; the publisher will probably display several ads while you try to read the article. I've found the quality of these to be poor at best.
- **Articles without references or quotes.** If an article you read neither quotes another source nor provides footnotes for further reading, take the content with a grain of salt and confirm elsewhere before you put too much stock in what was written.
- **Articles composed of lists.** These are very popular. Many times, each item in the list is displayed on a separate page. This is designed to show you more ads. Articles found on university web pages tend to be more accurate.

Newspapers. Even as newspapers get thinner and thinner, and regardless of your personal opinion on the political slant of printed media, reading a newspaper can give you knowledge of local news and world events. This knowledge gives you another topic to talk about with your spouse, something to discuss with friends, and a well-rounded view of the world. You need not be able to recite the name of every world leader, but it may be wise to know what is going on outside the four walls of your house.

Devotionals and Bible Study. Some people have been known to place short books or devotionals around their houses. Scatter a few books you want to read around the house; leave them on a bookcase in one room, a nightstand in another, the kitchen counter, and on the coffee table in the den. As you go throughout the day's cleaning, going to the bathroom, eating, or resting, you can stop and read a few sentences and then move on. Over the course of weeks, you will finish a book and can replace it with another one. Perhaps this technique could work for you!

Joining a regular Bible study group where a deeper understanding of the Bible can be gained works for some. Although a recurring meeting requires another slice of your time, it also creates a network where you can share your marriage and parenting concerns.

Learning in Marriage

Exceptional communication can assist you in your learning. There isn't enough time for you both to read every book; there may be a few you read aloud together at night or listen to together in the car, but for the most part, you'll have different reading lists. Plus, one of you is probably a more voracious reader than the other. Take a few minutes each day or week to talk about what you're reading and learning.

Communicate about the different breakout sessions you attend at conferences. Make sure to debrief about doctor's appointments and counseling sessions, even if both of you are in attendance. You will hear different messages, and your brains will highlight different thoughts. Also, trust each other with the knowledge being absorbed. You are smart, but in some cases, your spouse is going to have a stronger grip on facts and figures or on vision and tactics.

Aesop, the Greek storyteller, had it right. The tortoise's slow and steady movement wins the race! Having a college degree is not necessary to become a lifelong learner. We want you to always be learning, always be curious like a child, never be satisfied where you are, and always be keeping the welfare of your spouse and child at the forefront of your mind.

CHAPTER 17

CHOICES IN EDUCATION

*We must meet our students exactly where they are with
exactly the brains they have right now. We must use all
the tools we have available to us and not expect them to
fit into a mold or all behave exactly the same.*
—Dr. Gene R. Carter, former executive director of the Association
for Supervision and Curriculum Development

ROY

Think about a typical weekday for a special needs student during the
school year. Here is an example of what one such day might look like:

6:45 a.m.	Alarm goes off.
6:53 a.m.	Gets dressed. Eats breakfast. Takes meds.
7:21 a.m.	Drags self to the car.
7:23 a.m.	Heads back into the house to get forgotten homework.
7:26 a.m.	Rides to school in the back seat of the car.
7:48 a.m.	Jumps out of the car to catch up with a friend.
8:00 a.m.– 3:00 p.m.	School.

3:04 p.m.   Drags rolling backpack to car.

3:31 p.m.   Arrives one minute late for doctor's appointment.

4:37 p.m.   Remains quiet for a few minutes on the drive to the store.

4:43 p.m.   Rolls eyes while shopping with Mom.

5:03 p.m.   Brings groceries in from car.

5:09 p.m.   Opens refrigerator, searching for a snack.

5:11 p.m.   Begins homework.

5:14 p.m.   Takes a break.

5:17 p.m.   Dives into homework again.

5:57 p.m.   Finishes homework and picks up Wii controller.

6:19 p.m.   Goes outside under protest.

6:54 p.m.   Comes in for dinner.

7:21 p.m.   Whines about having to take a bath.

7:42 p.m.   Watches the bottom of the fifth inning with Dad.

8:18 p.m.   Takes meds and brushes teeth.

8:33 p.m.   Asks a dozen extra questions, delaying bedtime.

8:58 p.m.   Falls asleep.

Your child spends more time getting ready for, attending, coming home from, or doing homework from school than anything else in life. If you subtract sleep and school matters from a twenty-four-hour day, you'll see how little time you have to spend with your child, and you already know how hard it is to make that time effective and profitable.

How you educate your child is one of the toughest decisions you'll ever make.

Education is important! You and your spouse are ultimately the ones in charge of your child's education—not the local school board, not your school's principal, and not your child's teacher. The responsibility lies with parents.

How you educate your child is one of the toughest decisions you'll ever make. That decision is as individual as your child. Remember: the education needs of your child will change as your child matures. Puberty will have a major influence, as will a change in your child's diagnosis. This chapter will outline three categories of schooling and address some of the issues you'll face when making the right decision for your child. Above all, both parents have to be aligned in their approach to their child's education.

We had the realization some time ago that our children might not go to college. If they got through high school and were thinking about college, we'd find a way to finance it. We wanted to pull out all the stops during the critical high school years and make sure they were prepared for adulthood. For us, the best choice for two of our children became private school. The added horsepower to our efforts made a huge difference in some ways. Heather initially went to a private college preparatory school that we loved but in which she struggled; we ultimately transferred her to a private school for children with learning disabilities. This environment taught her how to advocate better for herself. The teachers focused on her dyslexia, and she prospered and graduated there. As Dylan went from eighth grade to tenth grade, private school became more and more challenging and the work load was too much for him to handle. We moved Dylan from private to public school so he could excel. When he was in eleventh grade in public school I clearly remember Dylan coming home and telling me the book they were reading was the same he had read in eighth grade in private school. He did much better finishing high school in a public school setting where the academic load was lighter and he was able to participate in other extracurricular activities. Molly was in the public school system for her entire education. We are proud that all have regular high school diplomas and throughout their education the choices we made were always made between the two of us and in our children's best interests.

Public Schools

Most families will find their children in public school. Public school systems have traveled lightyears in providing services to and making allowances for children with special needs. The creation of the IDEA and the addition of a trained staff make public schools, especially in larger areas, a fabulous fit.

Why Public School Might Be the Best for Your Child. Public education is paid for by the taxes collected from your area. While no education is truly free (there are still many fees and charges you'll experience in public school), the vast bulk of expenses are paid. In essence, the entire community works together to provide education for the next generation. By choosing public education for your child, you are maximizing your budget. Many public school systems provide transportation to and from the school, and many provide low-cost or free after-hours supervision of the students of working families. The money you save can be allocated for physicians and medications your child needs, as well as counseling opportunities. Additionally, public schools are held to federal standards provided by IEPs and the availability of M-team meetings, where all your child's teachers and parents come together to plot the course of their education. You have certain rights in the public school system that you may forfeit in private schools.

Why Public School Might Not Be for Your Child. Public school experiences vary drastically across our nation. Investigate your school to make sure systems, procedures, and opportunities are in place for your child. Although many services for disabled children are federally mandated, the school for which you're zoned may not be implementing them well. By placing your child in your local public school, you might have to become a leader in the drive to improve or demand improved special education services. There is no panacea in the educational arena. This is going to be hard work—not impossible, but truly hard.

Private Schools

Many communities are home to private schools that employ experts to run programs designed for children with special needs yet many have less experience in this area than public schools. Some private schools are live-in boarding schools, where your child might reside all year round. In our eyes, only a boarding school specializing in certain areas of learning disorders would be suitable for a special needs child. These children need supervision around the clock, and this is something that a boarding school generally cannot provide.

Why Private School Might Be the Best for Your Child. Private schools can be as expensive as many colleges yet for the college bound student this education can give them a head start into a university setting. Most private schools have classes with small student-to-teacher ratios and can closely monitor your child's behavior and academic progress. They will work with you to accomplish the goals you've set forth with your professional medical team and you may know the teachers more closely. Communication often is more direct and informal regarding your child's special needs where within the public school setting that communication can be more formalized with the child's IEP.

Why Private School Might Not Be for Your Child. Cost may be the overriding negative of a private school. Depending upon the specific school, some children are given more independence earlier. This may play to your child's disadvantage. If and when you investigate a private school, don't just look at the shiny best foot they put forward during tours and recruiting. Ask to speak with other parents and students. Ask about accommodations for special needs children and about what special needs children are already in the school. Ask to speak to the parents of special needs children attending the school. Attend a sporting event and watch how the students interact with each other. You want to ensure that the philosophy of the school is accepting of a diversity of children and that the other children are as well. Transportation to and special events at private schools also take more of your time to coordinate. As we discussed above, private school wasn't the best long term decision for all of our children, and it may not be for yours, but don't rule it out without considering or investigating it.

Homeschooling

Many families with special needs children choose to educate their children at home, hoping to tailor the curriculum and the pace of learning to the child's needs, learning style, and schedule. Educating at home also allows you ample time for taking the child to all of the doctor, psychiatrist, and counseling appointments necessary. Homeschooling is legal in all fifty states, but each state has its own set of laws and guidelines, which can make it tricky for families to navigate. The Homeschool Legal Defense Association is a clearinghouse for information about our nation's homeschooling laws, and it will have information for your state in particular. Their website (www.hslda.org) will help you research the laws for your state, the curricula available, and the number of families in your area who homeschool. Don't enter into homeschooling lightly! Open both eyes and learn the landscape so that you can make the best decision.

We realized that homeschooling would put us in the roles of both teacher and parent. This didn't work for us. Even our psychologists suggested that we should allow the school to do some of the fighting over homework and allow us to maintain our parental relationship with our children. Even after years of public and private schools, we sometimes feel like we've homeschooled our children anyway. We've taught the phases of the moon until we knew them by heart. We've both read *Watership Down* multiple times. We've done more projects than we did when we were in school, and we have read many history and science textbooks aloud to the children. We never want to touch modeling clay or build another bubbling volcano again in our lives. We always divided the subjects and independently tutored our children. Remember to use your strengths!

Homeschooling Options. At first blush, homeschooling may sound like setting up a classroom in a spare bedroom and teaching your child by yourself while adhering to a typical school day. Your child wakes up, eats breakfast, then reports for school, where they sit in a desk throughout the day as you go through subjects. In reality, though, if you walked into the houses of ten homeschooled families, you'd find a variety of setups.

Many children are involved in a homeschooling group of some kind. Every setup is unique. If you are considering homeschooling as an option, you may want to investigate cooperatives, umbrella schools, or tutorials. The internet is an excellent resource to find what homeschooling assistance is available in your area.

Why Homeschooling Might Be the Best or Worst for Your Child. Your child is unique. We mentioned above that homeschooling gives great flexibility in your schedule. If your child is in an intense season of therapy, homeschooling might make sense. If you're in a system now that isn't a good fit, you have the power at home to shape a customized system for your child and stimulate learning and thriving.

As a parent, you have to be switched on high alert when you are with your child. Homeschooling can create a great deal of fatigue for both parent and child. The close proximity to your child might get in the way of learning. You might spend too much time dealing with behavior or blowups, or you might be trying to get so much work done that you place your parent/child relationship in jeopardy. It might be better to have a teacher in your corner and for you to work with your child in the school system.

Socialization. Once you start asking around about homeschooling, you will hear the number-one objection, complaint, and fear: are homeschooled children socialized properly? Aren't they isolated and not properly connected with the community around them? The homeschooling community at large is committed to multigenerational interaction. Many homeschooled children have more advanced social skills and can talk more easily with adults, seniors, and children than with their peers. This is even true among children with psychological, educational, and developmental needs. Most homeschooling families operate a portion of their day in the "real world," which allows interaction in the marketplace and in the neighborhood. Community organizations like the public library, Human Society, nature centers, and museums have special events where homeschooled children can participate. These increase socialization in addition to providing unique learning opportunities. Many children who attend public or private school are *more* isolated than homeschooled children. Socialization, like most important matters in life, must be done with purpose and intention. Socialization can be done properly either in the public, private, or homeschool arena. Don't allow this to be your guiding principle in making a decision.

Relationships with Teachers and Administrators

Your child's teachers and tutors will become a part of your team. Each year, you must decide to trust them and bring them into your confidence. Share your challenges and hopes. Fill them in on what you're working on with your professional team. Put aside your own ego and the teacher's potential judgment. The teacher needs to know what you know! They have to control the classroom as well as focus on and teach your child. The more tools the teacher has, the more your child will thrive. Never, never cross your teacher's authority in front of your child. So many teachers have told us how much they appreciated our support and how open and frank we were in discussing the strengths and weaknesses of our children. They repeatedly told us how our discussions saved them time and allowed them to teach to our child's strengths.

In third grade, Heather was falling behind in her studies. Upon a visit to the classroom, Margrey suggested that if Heather's assignments were listed on the board, Heather might be able to follow them more closely. Her teacher tried this and found that *all* her students benefited from this small change in her teaching style. We hope you encounter many teachers that are this open to a small change in their classroom.

On the positive side, the administrator can be a strong advocate for your child. On the negative side, administrators have to reduce liability and think about the big picture for their school. They worry about everything from state rankings of test scores to the best use of the budget. Educating your child can be seen as weighing down both of these issues. They can become blinded to the needs of the few versus the needs of the many, and they may seek to reduce or eliminate programs that you find vital. However, they can be your greatest allies! The principal may see you as someone that pushes the county or city administration to up their game and provide more services within their school. This creates a winning environment for all the special needs children in that school system. You can fight the principal's battles with and for them. The special needs area won't be reported in the sports page, and your child and their classmates won't bring home trophies, but the principal will see the joy and hope in your eyes.

MARGREY

Extracurricular Activities and Sports

In talking with other parents of special needs children, Roy and I generally advise them to scale back on extracurricular activities. Families with children like ours are tempted to try and keep up with their extended families, friends at church, coworkers, and neighbors. However, you are all about raising your child to adulthood and independence. The chance of any child, much less a special needs child, being the next Michael Jordan or Steve Jobs is about the same as being struck by lightning this year: one in a million. Every child is different, and there are brilliant special needs children, but we feel a realistic attitude is essential.

We know much grief will occur here. You may have enjoyed playing sports growing up and dreamed of one day coaching your child's team. You will still have time to teach your child to ride a bicycle, but our experience was that organized extracurricular activities had to be limited for our overall success. All of our children participated in a sport at some point up to about the age of ten. Dylan was an accomplished pianist, and Heather loved the guitar. At some point, though, homework got harder, their attention spans became a roadblock, and their inability to focus on practice and the need to excel academically became frustrations for all of us. In every way, your child's story is different than every other child's. The time may come when your child can act in the school play or try out for cheerleading. You will celebrate these milestones, just as we have.

When it comes to your child's education—which dominates every day for many years—this must be a place where you are one with your spouse. You must be in total agreement about

- who will help with homework,
- how you measure success,
- what role grades will play, and
- how you will handle extracurricular activities.

If these areas aren't reconciled, you will spend too much energy fighting and not enough energy learning. You will spend remorseful time thinking you are a failure if your child doesn't excel. We found that with exceptional communication, acceptance of our children's strengths and weaknesses, and the help of teachers, we came to be just as proud—if not more so—of our children's educational achievements.

CHAPTER 18

EMERGING ADULTHOOD

For in every adult there dwells the child that was,
and in every child there lies the adult that will be.
—John Connolly, The Book of Lost Things

MARGREY

The goal for each of our children has been, and will continue to be, rearing them in a Christian environment so they grow to be godly individuals with a strong work ethic, emphasizing honesty and character, and preparing them to be committed marriage partners. We do not have specific life or career goals for them other than to be employed and have good self-esteem, derived in part from being contributing members of society. We recognize, though, that we can only do so much to form a good foundation. Much has to be done by the children themselves. We continue to trust God.

As your children enter the teen years and move into independent adulthood, you will encounter a new world. They begin making decisions on their own. They will fall, and you will pick them up again. If needed, and if you are lucky, they will allow you to coach them into maturity.

There are many bumps in the road as your special needs child grows and matures. We don't want to be negative, but we want you to be informed and educated. No individual does well when hit suddenly with difficult news or when learning of a situation that clearly comes out of the blue. There have been times when an unexpected incident comes from out of nowhere and is a complete shock to our family; it messes up the dynamics of our lives.

No matter how much you pregame and share with each other, something will happen—a medical diagnosis, a school situation, or a visit from a police officer. At this point, you won't believe what's happening in your life. What follows are several areas that can blindside you as your child moves into the late teen years and early adulthood. Some of these events, for many parents, have occurred much too early in their child's life, yet for the special needs family, you may be handling them later, as your child matures more slowly. All of this has the potential to create a wedge in your marriage if you are not alert.

Friendships and Dating

As you are aware, all children mature at different ages. The special needs child may be much slower in their maturation, and their behavior can be inappropriate for their age. Many times, a special needs child becomes ostracized from their peers, and their friendships can be limited; what friendships they have can deteriorate easily. A special needs child may have less self-awareness or less ability to read the body language and social cues of those around them. This can easily become a source of tension among peers. Even the parents of your child's friends may be uncomfortable managing your child. For this reason, we tended to host parties at our house, where we could maintain some semblance of social control.

Our children actually interacted well with adults at social functions, so we took them to many community events and dental conventions.

We took bike trips around the local university campus on weekends, and we would walk around town, generally ending up at the ice cream shop. For many years, we hosted end-of-year school parties at our home. We traveled and visited family often. None of these activities were without stress and drama, but we were committed to our children. They needed to be exposed to life and society. It would have been easier just to stay home and let them watch TV all the time, but that was not our idea of either family time or appropriate parenting.

As children enter the adolescent years, the expectations for them to mature increase. Some special needs children can't keep up. They are socially inappropriate in the most awkward ways. Molly has asked multiple pregnant ladies if they had sex to get pregnant. At twenty-five, she is finally realizing this is not appropriate. Although an adult can negotiate these outbursts, other teens do not have the skills to do so, and your child gets ostracized—sometimes unintentionally. It is difficult to create a safe social life for many special needs children. Be especially aware that when your special needs child runs in circles with peers their own chronological age, they may also be easy targets for sexual exploitation due to their social immaturity.

Professional Counseling

All of our children have been under the care of a psychiatrist for most of their lives. There comes a point in a teen's maturity when they realize that all their friends are not also seeing a psychiatrist. They begin to stand out when they have so many medical appointments. They start wanting to be as normal as everyone else. They may start fighting taking medications or pushing back on psychology appointments. Lastly, just like you, they may grow tired of all the appointments and special medications. Start early in their life by emphasizing repeatedly that this is part of their life and their ability to succeed. Communication with your child is as important as communication with your spouse.

Cell Phones and the Internet

Lucky us, we got to parent just when cell phones became affordable for everyone. "All my friends have a cell phone," Heather constantly told us. "You don't want me to be stuck somewhere that I can't reach you guys and I need help!" We had no rules to guide us. The doctors didn't have much advice, since it was such a new technology. We tend to parent on the conservative side when it comes to new situations, so we watched and listened to other parents trying to deal with this development.

In the end, our children had cell phones, but much later than their peers. Our rule was that cell phones were put in our bathroom at 9:00 p.m. to charge and stayed there all night. Cell phones were not allowed at the dinner table and never taken to school.

If educators, doctors, and parents could all get together, they might eliminate access to the internet for any given child. As businesspeople and mature adults, we cherish the access to information the internet provides. There are so many things on the internet to make our lives more efficient! But mature adults can usually handle the internet, whereas in the hands of any child, it can be a scary scenario.

Parents struggle with typical children on a daily basis with technology, trying to set boundaries, teach right from wrong, and prevent anyone from hurting their children. For our special needs children, who often make poor judgment decisions and aren't even aware of the evil world that exists around them, it is a total nightmare. We finally had to lock our office where our computers are located. We tried to sit with Molly during computer time, but in an instant, she could move to an inappropriate site just out of curiosity.

Another thing about computers is that it appears as if all children are born with a computer chip in their brain. Even children with special needs in this day and age have grown up as computer natives. As computer savvy as Margrey and I were, the skills they instantly developed with the computer and internet were overwhelming to us. Start early on with monitoring and limiting computer access. This is another area for you to keep learning so you can stay abreast of their knowledge.

Driving

In our household, Roy took the lead in teaching driving skills, although none of our children were ever that interested in learning how to drive. Our doctors told us that children with ADHD find driving to be a frightening experience. My children would talk to me while I was driving and acknowledge that they didn't know how I could do it with all those cars coming at me all the time. It was always interesting to listen to my children, because they saw the world from such a different view. My world is full of black and white, with rules and benchmarks. Their world was often filled with color and music and patterns. So, when teaching your child to drive, think outside the box, and don't plan on teaching them the same way *you* were taught.

> *Children with ADHD find driving to be a frightening experience.*

Roy was always taking the children to the church parking lot to practice driving. They still talk about his rule for a stop sign: he had to feel the car gently roll backward after a full and complete stop, and then they could look for other cars before proceeding. Since no one was that interested in driving, we decided that we had to encourage them a little, or I would be driving them around for the rest of my life. We insisted that Heather and Dylan go to driving school when they were eighteen, and as adults, they have excellent driving records. Molly still has no desire to drive (at least legally).

Learning Self-Advocacy

When your child turns fourteen, the school system will ask to include them in the IEP process. This is usually the first step into self-advocacy for your child. You have the right to decide whether to include your child or not. According to the IDEA law, the school system has to bring this matter up with you. Remember, *you* control most of what occurs at an IEP meeting.

At some point, your children will start to ask questions like, "What is wrong with me?" or, "Why do I have to keep going to the doctor?" or maybe even, "Why has God done this to me?" All of them are good questions, and you will have to come to terms with your answers. We tried in simple terms to explain what ADHD is and how they will cope. We told them that it will be a long-term issue and that we would always be there for them. We also explained that as they get older and a little wiser, we may not be there for them, and that they need to learn how to be independent. This doesn't necessarily mean living on their own, but it does mean that they learn to be as independent as they can be in all aspects of their lives. Most children learn by doing. As parents, we have to eventually let go so they can learn and explore. Our overarching goal was to keep their errors small and avoid any life-changing mistakes.

Failure after failure can lead to frustration, but each failure has the potential to be another teaching moment. You can use your psychologist to help your family navigate these emotions. The children have to come to terms with the fact that they have a chronic illness or condition. My life as a physical therapist has proved to me that many people function quite well in the world despite a chronic illness or handicap. Because I have lupus, I use that as a way to connect with the kids when explaining the way things are for them. I tell them that we don't have to like our condition or illness, but we do have to get to the point of accepting it. Usually, I tell them that their lives will improve when they learn acceptance. When your children go to college or live independently, you have to really stress to them the importance of taking their medications regularly and on time. They will need you to help think through some strategies with them. Create an atmosphere of family, and look out for each other like wolves in a pack. We advocate for each other all the time, because we care.

Conservatorship

The things your special needs child does or says may be cute at age ten or twelve, but as they reach more recognized ages of maturity, those things become intrusive into other people's lives. At age eighteen, legal issues may arise. What do you do? Luckily for us, we had an older, wise psychiatrist who had seen the good, bad, and ugly of life and gave us wonderful counsel on this matter. I can still hear him say to me, "Ms. Thompson, I don't want anything terrible to happen to Molly and you have to deal with the aftermath." Good thing I listened.

The psychiatrist recommended for all my children that the day they turn eighteen, we create a celebration for them at the attorney's office. In advance, we made a big deal out of going to the attorney's office, and soon after their eighteenth birthday, off we went. At eighteen, they got their own appointment with the family attorney to sign a simple will, a power of attorney, and a health care power of attorney. Every child signed with no problems, except for signing the will. They would say, "I have no money to leave to anybody, and why would I want to leave it to my siblings?" When you hear comments like this, you must remember that whether or not they have special needs, they are still only eighteen years old.

Molly's case was different. For her, the doctors recommended a conservatorship. To obtain a conservatorship, you go before a judge with your child's medical records and letters of recommendation from the psychiatrist to present the case that your child cannot make decisions on their own and they are incompetent to make adult decisions. The ease of this task varies from state to state, and you will need an attorney to help you negotiate the system. In our case, the judge had several detailed questions to ask us. My husband and I are coconservators for our daughter, Molly, and her sister serves as assistant conservator. Our thinking behind this process was that if Roy and I died in an accident on the same day or so, our daughter Heather would be able to step in immediately, without anyone having to take action at the courthouse.

As conservator of Molly, once a year I'm required by law to present a financial report plus any change of address or circumstances to the court authorities. I learned from experience that this filing is critical and must be timely. The first year, I was about a week late in filing the report because I was trying to get the financial information down to the exact penny. I received a letter from the judge asking me if there was a problem and to get the report in to his office.

A conservatorship helps to mitigate the consequences of actions that an adult would usually be considered competent to make but your child may not be fully equipped to understand. In the blink of an eye, these young adults can get themselves into trouble, even when you are standing right beside them. Our experience with cell phone carriers is so long that when you pull up my family account to this day, it flashes in bright red like, "Beware!" We carry a copy of the conservatorship paperwork in my purse and Roy's backpack, and each car has a copy in the glove compartment. Close friends have a copy in their personal safe in case they need to assist our children in a worst-case scenario. We never travel without a copy of Molly's conservatorship documents.

One time we were returning from a cruise with eight people in our party, including Roy's elderly mother. Roy was trying to locate eight-plus bags in the Customs and Immigration area, and I was hanging onto my mother-in-law when I heard my name. I looked up to see security officers interrogating Molly, about to detain her. Roy looked like he was doing jumping jacks, screaming my name. As I ran over to security, I whipped out the conservatorship papers, not knowing exactly what was going on. Molly had been taking photos in a place where multiple signs clearly said, "No photos in this area." Once we explained that Molly had learning issues and showed them her conservatorship paperwork, the problem became nominal. Molly got a bit of a lecture and was told her camera could be confiscated, but in the end, disaster was averted. The same thing happened with our cell phone carrier. Once they realized that Molly cannot enter into a legal contract, our account was handled, and the phone Molly had ordered was returned.

I know of problems from other parents who didn't get this administrative/legal work done and encountered nightmares. We have an acquaintance who didn't get a conservatorship. Their son ordered a car online, and it was delivered to their home. They got that crisis straightened out, and the son did it all over again on another website. That child is now in his early twenties and gaining a conservatorship is much more difficult. If you plan to appeal to the court for a conservatorship, we feel the sooner after your child's eighteenth birthday that you apply the better off you will be. The ability to obtain a conservatorship varies by states yet a conservatorship, where appropriate, can give you peace of mind and protect your child.

We have another acquaintance whose adult child developed mental health problems and was hospitalized. Since she was twenty-three years old, the doctor could not discuss her health care with her parents because they did not have health care power of attorney. Like I said earlier, I appreciate how much our children's psychiatrists have helped my entire family over the years.

Long-Term Planning

There is no particular year when your special needs child is a fully mature adult. Remember, everyone's ruler is different. Many young adults with special needs are able to enter a local vocational rehabilitation program for assessment of their working skills. Some communities have sheltered workshops for jobs for special needs adults. Often, parents are able to reach out to stores or companies in their hometown to look for jobs for their child. These are typically only part-time positions. It requires dedication on behalf of the parents to keep up with schedules and get their child to and from work, but the joy, excitement, and pride these maturing adults receive is overwhelming. They get their life dream—to be just like all their friends.

We are also aware of parents' decisions to place their maturing special needs child in an independent living situation like an apartment. We have seen this fail more often than succeed. In our opinion, this is highly risky and must be completely evaluated prior to making this decision. Without a highly structured day, the immature adult often eats improperly, leading to weight gain that can have lifelong consequences. They may tend to watch television or play video games for hours on end. More seriously, due to their immaturity or delayed intellect, they are targets for financial or sexual exploitation.

All parents would like to plan for the safety and satisfaction of their child for their entire life. This is an impossible task. Part of everyone's growth involves making mistakes and growing independently. Yet for the child that may never mature, as parents, we need to have some sort of life-long plan in place so that upon our death, our child's life moves forward. Hopefully, your child has siblings or cousins who, as they mature, would step up and take responsibility for your child's care. Potentially, an aunt or uncle or close friend can act as their guardian.

Long-term planning like this continues to be unsettling to us and probably will be for some time. It is imperative that you give some direction to your family as you age so you don't leave family members and your child in a critical situation. We talk to God about this problem continually. Our prayer to Him is that He keep our children safe and secure after we are gone. This is where faith steps in; we trust God with our children and ask Him to empower those responsible for our children to make good decisions with wisdom, grace, and love.

As your child moves into adulthood, you lose some control. Realize this will come, and work with your spouse ahead of time to have some idea of how to handle this new phase of your child's life. There is not a cookbook for this process. We trust we have alerted you to some issues you will face. Communication, planning, and prayer will get you through.

CHAPTER 19

FINDING JOY

Strengthened with all might, according to his glorious power,
unto all patience and longsuffering with joyfulness.
—*Colossians 1:11 (King James Version)*

MARGREY

After having read eighteen possibly overwhelming chapters, it is time for you to refocus on the joy that any child can bring to the lives of their parents. You have heard our stories and sensed some of our frustrations, but we couldn't ask for a more joyful experience than being challenged by the special circumstances that come with our three wonderful children.

> *We couldn't ask for a more joyful experience than being challenged by the special circumstances that come with our three wonderful children.*

Many couples over the years have expressed sorrow or sadness over what we were managing with our children. We never accepted these emotions. It wasn't right, and it was never how we felt. As a strong couple, Roy and I believe that God sent Heather, Dylan, and Molly to us because He had a purpose for them and for us. No matter how difficult or taxing our situation, we never wavered from this belief.

The entire experience of twenty-five to thirty years has been humbling and brought us to tears and our knees many times, but it has all been with great reward. The turning point in parenting my children came one night when Molly was about five years old. Remember, Molly has a severe lack of communication skills and the ability to express emotions and even has trouble understanding what we are trying to communicate and teach her. It was nighttime, and Molly was having a full-blown meltdown. In these times, it required me pinning her down on her bed or the floor to restrain her from hurting herself or me or damaging something in the house. She was crying and screaming, but I knew from prior experience that by holding her down, I could help her regain physical and emotional control of herself. At the same time she was crying, I too was crying, out of frustration. I felt like I was trying to train an animal instead of rearing a child. I prayed out loud to God for help. My prayer was simple. "Teach me, God, what to do for Your child, Molly, made in Your image." Over and over, like a mantra, I cried out to God.

I realize that no one alive has seen God, but seated on that tiny twin bed, I felt God's presence and enormous peace. At that split second, I realized that God would walk this path of parenting with us day in and day out, and I shouldn't be afraid. Molly became peaceful and so did I, and the feeling of God's presence has never left me. It changed my attitude toward my parenting role, and I started to see the joy in the work I was doing on a daily basis.

I ignored advice people gave me, except for that of the psychiatrist and psychologist. Yes, I even ignored my own parents' advice. I knew who to listen to on a regular basis. I started thinking like a physical therapist again, as I had been professionally trained. I recognized Molly's deficits and created plans to overcome or minimize them. Progress was slow, but with Roy beside me, we did make progress.

As I read my Bible, I gained a new perspective on the word perseverance as described in Hebrews 12:1–2 (NIV): "And let us run with perseverance the race marked out for us, fixing our eyes on Jesus, the pioneer and perfecter of faith."

The joy that has come from parenting three special needs children is unique. First, you have to develop the skill of delayed gratification. While your friends may be bragging about developmental milestones, athletic achievements, and academic successes, you have to learn to tune all of that out of your brain. If your child is making progress in whatever area or deficits they are working on at school or at home, you have a winner, and you as a parent get a gold star for that day. Please realize that there are not many parents who can do your job day in and day out and keep a positive attitude. Many parents just give up or push their child onto someone else and hope for the best. Those that endure are the champions!

We had a psychologist once who told us that we really didn't need his services. He said that Roy and I generally came up with novel ways of handling our children's behavioral issues and that his job was to clap, praise, and continue encouraging us to keep going and just not give up on the children. His role was to encourage us so we were energized to encourage the children.

Today, after thirty-one years of parenting, I see the results of all our tedious work. My children are nice, kind, respectful adults who still have their special needs. They are loving and compassionate to their friends and us. No one has married yet, but our oldest is engaged to a lovely young man. Dylan is finishing his senior year in college after a stint in the US Army, and Molly, our youngest, lives and works out of state in a program training its clients for independent living and life skills.

They have jobs, live independently, can manage daily finances, and vote on a regular basis. All could attend church more frequently. They are busy living their own lives. Roy and I couldn't be happier, even when they appear to be too busy to talk to us. It is another sign that their lives are moving forward, which we see as a success. They are living happy, successful lives, where they are as safe as they can possibly be in the world. James 1:2–3 (NIV) tells us, "Consider it pure joy, my brothers and sisters, whenever you face trials of many kinds, because you know that the testing of your faith produces perseverance."

You will only grow stronger, as an individual and as a married couple, from this wild and challenging life of rearing special needs children. Consider it a privilege and these children as a gift from God. Two things always kept me going on a daily basis:

1. Keep my eyes on Jesus.
2. Continue knowing that if God didn't think we could do this job, He wouldn't have given these children to us.

Keep loving your spouse and your children, even though some days you may feel your children are unlovable. These thoughts are normal. I admit that I hated having these thoughts, but I always kept loving my children. Realize that there is peace with God through your faith. I often felt alone and isolated. This is why communication with your spouse through daily debriefing is so vital to your success.

If God didn't think we could do this job, He wouldn't have given these children to us.

In Romans 5:3–5, Paul talks about rejoicing in our suffering. On my hardest days, my attempt was always to rest assured my trials would be rewarded. Looking back on the suffering of parenting these children can produce endurance, that endurance can build your character, and that character produces hope. Hope is what all parents share on behalf of these children—hope for your children's health, their ability to be productive citizens of their community, and for them to be faithful Christians with gainful employment, joyful marriages, and fruitful lives. All parents share these hopes, but sometimes with special needs children, the movement is slow. We have to keep the faith; stand tall and strong with your spouse, knowing you have a partner in this battle.

In your journey, never forget also to celebrate the small successes. Football players don't just celebrate at the end of the game. After every great run or tackle, you will see the players pumping their fists in exuberant celebration. As a parent, you must keep this same focus on small successes. Highlight the one good grade your child got this grading period. Acknowledge them for the one time they get out of bed on time for school. It is easy to get worn down. Stop and take an assessment so you can see the progress you are making and can celebrate in your nightly debrief.

Our continued hope is that you will meet a level of success and find pure joy in the successes of your children. Delight in the joy of your children and in yourself. You have learned how to live a worthy life, and this will add a great deal to your character. Remember to smile and share a laugh with your family! Rejoice!

EPILOGUE

ROY

You will, in your own way, survive raising your special needs child, and we hope you have an outstanding and enchanting marriage. Your specific successes will be measured by your own ruler. For your child, educational success might be graduating from high school. Perhaps technical school or college will be realistic. Many children with developmental, psychological, or educational needs will grow up to be employed according to their level of ability. Other children may transition to an adult residential center. Because of the enormous time investment you are making, your child may even function better than so-called "normal" children, because they have lived a more structured and supervised life and may be less likely to rebel in their late teens. You are building a strong bond with your spouse. You and your spouse are standing back to back to fend off the world. You continue eliminating roadblocks that may keep you from being partners. You are finding real strength and meaning in those words spoken years ago: "In good times and bad, for richer or poorer, in sickness and health, till death do us part."

There are times you may have wanted to take your child's antianxiety medications yourself so you could be calmer. Margrey told the psychologist at one appointment, "Either you medicate *her*, or you medicate *me*!"

She came home after that visit and leaned on me for support. She has leaned on me countless times, and I have leaned on her. Many times, the things we heard about our children made us uncertain of the future. It hasn't been easy, but here we are today: still married, still happy, still smiling. Our desire is for you to have similar success in your marriage.

Hopefully your children will find their way and move on—I mean, actually *move out*. Although many will not be independent very rapidly, they will function on their own. God may choose to guide them to spouses with characteristics that complement their weaknesses, or God may choose for them to live as single individuals with extra time to care for themselves. Just as in every family, some children will boomerang occasionally and land back on your porch temporarily. But as a married couple, you *will* regain your domain. Your house *will* be quiet. You will miss your child, but you will also cherish the peace and quiet that permeates your home.

And then, they all come home at once. Having special needs children back in the house after they have moved out takes us back to a time when

This is our *family*.

we had to parent 24/7. We unconditionally love our children and cherish their return, but when the three of them get together back in our house, the progress they have made sometimes vanishes, and they revert to third-grade behavior. They are in their twenties and thirties now, and we want them to have more understanding and patience. We want them to show outward love and compassion to each other. We want them to be mature. Instead, they pick on each other, they roll their eyes, and they make snide comments. I actually love it, because this is family. This is *our* family. God has blessed us with these children. I have been blessed with a spouse who will walk, run, and crawl with me as we take steps toward success in raising our children. I love the times when the kids come home, because there can be especially touching moments—like when a child opens a Christmas gift from a sibling and then jumps up to give them a hug. There are moments to cherish when a child offers gratitude for advice we have given them or when we have deep conversations about their futures. There are early mornings when we share a cup of coffee and late evenings when we have a glass of wine.

Whether our children are at home or away, every single night, Margrey and I retreat to the solace of our bedroom, where a pillow-top mattress, nice cotton sheets, a fluffy comforter, and the perfect pillows await the nighttime recap of our progress. Never perfection, always progress.

So, my dear friends, go to bed tired and sleep soundly. Tomorrow comes quickly.

LETTER TO A HURTING WIFE

MARGREY

Do you feel alone in your marriage? Do you feel like your husband sees little value in the hours you spend serving him and your children? Do you feel like you shoulder the bulk of the load of your child's needs and treatment? Do you feel he's more like the southbound end of a northbound horse? Do you feel invisible?

You are *not* alone.

In our conversations with wives throughout the years, we've seen the worry lines and heard the stress in voices. We've offered tissues for the tears. You picked up this book out of a mix of desperation and hope; as you begin to read, you might throw the book across the room because you think that your husband can't make those commitments to you.

Don't give up hope.

Express your love and commitment to him. The reasons you married him have not gone away or been destroyed. They are just obscured by the realities of life. He may be hurting too. He shows his pain and reacts to circumstances in different ways than you do.

Be patient. Be gracious. Every fiber of your being may want to lash out. There may be a time for a raised voice, but on most occasions, patience will win.

Invite him to engage every night. We discuss the importance of "pre-gaming" and "debriefing." These are essential tools for you. Start communicating about doctor's appointments, challenges you see, and the family schedule each night. Discuss what scares you about your child or even yourself. Share your thoughts and fears openly.

Invite your husband to attend marital counseling with you. As you will read throughout this book, we are firm believers in professional help. Don't wait. Get started this week. If he refuses, go alone. Keep going, and keep gently and lovingly inviting him to go with you. Learn what you can, and share the lessons with him gently.

Practice the key principles of this book anyway. We want your marriage to endure—and grow stronger—for the long haul. This book is written to help you work together to have a rich marriage and raise children as a team. In your situation, you might be traveling alone for a time. Think about driving on the interstate during a rainstorm; experts tell us that you should slow down, turn on your hazard lights, and keep driving. You will be traveling faster than the storm, and you will exit it soon. Sometimes storm clouds sit over an area for a long time. If you pull over, you could be rocked by the storm for a long time. If you feel alone, you are in a storm. Don't stop. Don't give up. Drive on.

Find a tough but nurturing friend to walk with you. It may take you a while to find another woman to walk with you. She has to be safe, be able to put up with you, and be willing to get her hands dirty. If you want her to share your life, you will need to take risks with what you say and practice great transparency. Both of you will have to keep each other's strictest confidence. This will be a friend that will be honest and straightforward with you. Sometimes it is tough to look into the mirror and see how our own expectations and behavior may be part of the problem. Be thoughtful as you look for this friend.

Don't give up. You endured childbirth or the long process of paperwork for an adoption. *You can do this.* Your husband will join you. When he does, value his thoughts, even though he may lack experience. In some things he will be naïve and shortsighted yet stay committed and hopefully he will come to join you equally in this effort.

Believe in God. We've always believed that our children were a gift directly from God. They are also God's children, and they are made in His image. Our bottom-line statement is that God would not have sent these children to us if He didn't think we could do the job of loving them and rearing them. At some point in our journey, we quit feeling sorry for ourselves and got busy working. You are capable of this also. Regardless of your past relationship with God, you need a friend like Him beside you on this journey. Trust that a higher power is at work in your life and a greater purpose in life lies ahead for you and your family.

We wrote this book without apology and with a hopeful, optimistic tone. Don't take that as an attempt to sweep your painful reality under the couch! We just know firsthand that life is richer when we keep focusing our eyes on even one good thing rather than many hardships. The trials are real, but so are the good things. Keep finding the positive in life, and be grateful for even small things.

LETTER TO A FRUSTRATED HUSBAND

ROY

Look, as a husband, I get it. Life is difficult. You work hard for your family every day. You feel like you have no time alone with your frazzled wife. You don't remember the last time you made love (or, unfortunately, you *do* remember, and it's been a while). You don't have any time to yourself or with your friends. When you have time for your children, you are so tired you fall asleep reading them a book at bedtime. Above all else, you don't see any end in sight for your child's needs. You may be thinking, "This is not how I envisioned marriage and parenting. This is not what I signed up for!"

Don't give up hope. Don't give up on your wife, don't give up on your children, and by all means, don't give up on yourself.

Forgive yourself and offer your compassion to her. Be honest with yourself. No matter how hard you try, if you are the average father, you know less about your child's diagnosis and day-to-day struggles than your wife does. The vast majority of women get the lion's share of day-to-day childcare activities. That's okay! Her load is heavy. Yet you need not beat yourself up over this. She needs a soft voice, understanding, and strong shoulders. You can work together in many ways to help carry her load.

She needs you to be strong for her. Your children need a strong father figure in their lives.

Walk a mile in her shoes. Give her a day and night off to catch up on sleep. If money is tight, send her off to spend the night with one of her girlfriends. She needs sleep, a good meal or two, and the chance to escape into a novel or a few episodes of a TV show she hasn't seen in a year. She will return refreshed, and you'll be reminded of so many things you've taken for granted. Write them down, share them with her when she returns, and express exactly how grateful you are for everything she does.

Adopt two phrases: "What can I do?" and "Help me understand." "What can I do?" is a powerful question. When your wife is expending energy on you, the kids, or the upkeep of the home, don't stand idly by. Many men think that their contribution is mostly their paycheck, even when their wives work too. Ask, "What can I do?" and when the answer comes, accept it as a call for assistance. Get to work! You may also see things that you know need to be done. Just take care of them and communicate about them during your nightly talks. Caution: Don't brag or expect a pat on the back. Let accomplishment be its own reward.

When she is frazzled by your child's needs, the schedule, the bills, worry, her career, or more, she might have an edge when she talks with you. Address her with compassion: "Help me understand what you're feeling." I know how hard it is to let hurtful comments go. You're a man. Nobody talks to you that way. With your wife, however, bite your lip and seek to understand what's going on in her world.

Lead. If your wife bought this book and gave it to you to read, resist being offended. Sure, she may handle more tasks with your special needs child, but she needs you to be involved and to lead. Put these principles into effect in your home. God placed you as the head of your household for this purpose. More than once, we've heard that repeating the same actions and expecting different results is the definition of insanity. If what you're doing is not working well, try some of what has worked well for us.

Also, don't get stuck in the same place. Try something different. Step up and be a leader in your family.

Communicate your love and commitment. Your wife needs to know you stand with her no matter what comes down the pike. Tell her, "I love you," every morning and evening. Never leave for work without kissing her goodbye. Figure out what speaks to her heart and how she hears your special love. Every day, tell her—and show her in ways meaningful to her—how much you love her. Help her feel that you *meant* "for better and for worse" in your marriage vows. She needs to know with absolute confidence that you are not going to desert her and the children.

Defend her. The world has each of you in the crosshairs. Think about it: teachers, doctors, nurses, pharmacists, fellow shoppers, members of your church, and even your family will say hurtful things and offer their opinions. Your spouse is putting out fires all day long, every day. I know she's tough as nails, but this isn't a movie. You don't stand aside and marvel at her martial arts and fighting skills as she takes on the world! At a minimum, fight beside her, but sometimes, you'll need to step between her and the thing coming at her. Let her tap out. Defending her also means praising her for the battles she fights alone; but be careful, and don't assume a particular battle is over. Defending her may take you to different battlefields, including doctor's offices, grocery store aisles, family Christmas parties, and parent/teacher conferences.

Don't give up. What is the toughest task or issue you've faced? Major illness or injury? Military deployment? Losing a job? Whatever it is, you are still here; so you do have the power within you to succeed. You can do this! You're a man. Act like one. As the saying goes, "Man up!"

We wrote this book without apology and with a hopeful, optimistic tone. We know life isn't always rosy. That is our reality also. We have lived it, just like you are living it. I have held my wife when she was crying and held my tongue when she was yelling at me. This is a fight, and you've got to know who the real enemy is and remember the reason you're fighting. This book is primarily about keeping a strong marriage.

You're stronger than you think you are. You have more fuel in your tank. Don't give up.

We've spoken to too many parents who have separated because of the stress of rearing children. We've seen too many children take on the grief of loss when divorce occurs. We want you and your spouse to be a team that is unstoppable. Every team has a leader; lead with positivity, engagement, and happiness. Do it because when the children are gone, the two of you are left as best friends, lovers, and marriage partners, with memories that will carry you throughout your long life together.

LETTER TO A SINGLE PARENT

The irony isn't lost on us. You picked up a *marriage* book, as you navigate your journey as a single parent with a special needs child. The twists and turns of *your* parenting are exponentially more complicated and heart-wrenching than *ours*. Under the best circumstances, we feel like we *rarely* get a break. You *never* do.

Many single parents like you have swapped stories with us. Each time we part ways, we marvel at their strength and will to fight. We also grieve over their exhaustion.

Don't give up hope.

Glean what you can and throw away the rest. Many chapters focus on collaboration between spouses and how to parent together. Skim those parts and dig into the parenting advice throughout. You'll be like a quality control inspector. You'll say things like, "This one's good; that's one's a reject" . . . "I can use this" . . . "Are you kidding me with this one?" Your highlighter will be your best friend as you read.

Your team is essential. We will discuss how to build a team of medical experts. Build your team now, if you don't already have one, and strengthen it quickly if you do. You will find a network of similar-minded friends. As a solo parent, you must lean on friends and family.

Evaluate your church. Many churches are doing excellent work in reaching out to special needs families. Is yours? If not, prayerfully consider making a change. Likewise, many churches have expanded their ministries to single parents. If your church is strong in both areas, you will have a powerful home base. If you like your present church family—and if you have the energy—consider starting a support group or new ministry in your own church. The relationships you create could make a huge difference for you and change the lives of other families.

Find a tough but nurturing friend to walk with you. Margrey has a dear friend who went through a tough marital separation and ultimately a divorce. Margrey became her sounding board. She would call Margrey, sometimes late at night, to vent about the emotional experiences she and her children were having with so many issues. Her hurt and frustration was apparent. Her fear for her children and their futures was obvious. Usually, she would reach her own solutions and decisions by just voicing them out loud. Margrey was just the calm observer and focused listener. Their relationship has lasted for decades and she is now in a solid place. I remember her once telling me, "Margrey, was the only thing that saved me during those long days. She was blunt and kept pushing me toward resolving my feelings and moving into the future."

It may take you a while to find the right person to walk with you. He or she has to be safe, be willing to put up with you, and be willing to get her hands dirty. You want this intimate and private relationship with a trusted friend to be honest and open. You will have to practice great transparency, and both of you will have to keep each other's strictest confidence. Be prayerful as you look for this person. We offer one word of caution as you search for this friend and confidant: your child is not the person to turn to for help. Your child needs to grow up without the burden of the load you carry. Whatever you do, remember that your son or daughter is your child, not your best friend.

Don't give up. You're more resilient than you know. God has not brought you here to fail. He will give you the strength you need, in twenty-four-hour installments, to love your child and endure the challenges. Trust God. Talk to Him nonstop. He will never desert you.

We wrote this book without apology and with a hopeful, optimistic tone. Don't take that as an attempt to sweep your painful reality under the rug! We just know firsthand that life is richer when we keep moving our eyes to see even one good thing rather than focusing on the parts of life and parenting that really stink. Choosing optimism focuses your eyes and heart on the good. Keep discovering the good things about this life and your wonderful child.

THOMPSON FAMILY VALUES

Follow the Ten Commandments.

Go to school or work unless you are vomiting or running a fever.

Always be honest with each other.

Always do your best.

Eat dinner together at the table every night.

Always continue talking with each other.

Go to church together on Sunday morning.

We always stand behind our children.

You do the crime, you pay the time.

Take responsibility for your actions.

What part of "NO" do you not understand?

You are a Thompson, so behave by our family standards.

RECOMMENDED READING

Are You Fully Charged? The 3 Keys to Energizing Your Work and Life by Tom Rath

Brave: 50 Everyday Acts of Courage to Thrive in Work, Love and Life by Margie Warrell

Die Empty: Unleash Your Best Work Every Day by Todd Henry

Eat That Frog!: Great Ways to Stop Procrastinating and Get More Done in Less Time by Brian Tracy

Emotional Intelligence: Why It Can Matter More Than IQ by Daniel Goleman

The 5 Love Languages: The Secret to Love That Lasts by Gary Chapman

The Holy Bible (any version!)

Mindless Eating: Why We Eat More Than We Think by Brian Wansink

No Excuses!: The Power of Self-Discipline by Brian Tracy

The Power of Full Engagement: Managing Energy, Not Time, Is the Key to High Performance and Personal Renewal by Jim Loehr and Tony Schwartz

The Power of Story: Rewrite Your Destiny in Business and in Life by Jim Loehr

Rest: Why You Get More Done When You Work Less by Alex Soojung-Kim Pang

The 7 Habits of Highly Effective People: Powerful Lessons in Personal Change by Stephen R. Covey

The 3 Big Questions for a Frantic Family: A Leadership Fable about Restoring Sanity to the Most Important Organization in Your Life by Patrick Lencioni

Why Marriages Succeed or Fail: And How You Can Make Yours Last by John Gottman

Younger Next Year: Live Strong, Fit, and Sexy—Until You're 80 and Beyond by Chris Crowley and Henry S. Lodge

RESOURCES FOR DEALING
WITH YOUR CHILD'S SPECIAL NEEDS

Answers to Distraction by Edward M. Hallowell, MD, and John J. Ratey, MD

Attention Deficit Hyperactivity Disorder: State of Science Best Practices by Peter S. Jensen and James R. Cooper

The Bipolar Child: The Definitive and Reassuring Guide to Childhood's Most Misunderstood Disorder by DemitrI Papolos, MD, and Janice Papolos

The Defiant Child: A Parent's Guide to Oppositional Defiant Disorder by Dr. Douglas A. Riley

Driven to Distraction: Recognizing and Coping with Attention Deficit Disorder by Edward M. Hallowell, MD, and John J. Ratey, MD

The Out-of-Sync Child: Recognizing and Coping with Sensory Processing Disorder by Carol Stock Kranowitz, MA

Parenting a Child with Attention Deficit/Hyperactivity Disorder by Jane Hannah

Taking Charge of ADHD: The Complete, Authoritative Guide for Parents by Russell A. Barkley, PhD

Understanding Dyslexia: A Practical Approach for Parents and Teachers by Anne Marshall Huston, EdD

Wrightslaw: No Child Left Behind by Peter W. D. Wright, Esq., Pamela Darr Wright, and Suzanne Whitney Heath

Your Defiant Child: Eight Steps to Better Behavior by Russell A. Barkley, PhD, and Christine M. Benton

CPSIA information can be obtained
at www.ICGtesting.com
Printed in the USA
LVHW111133180820
663480LV00004B/217